To my loveliest and d
Shobana,

Thank you for being
Love you,
N

BRIDGING CULTURES

THE GUIDE TO SOCIAL INNOVATION IN COSMOPOLITAN CITIES

DR. NOHA NASSER

ISBN-13: 978-1517157180

PUBLISHED BY:
10-10-10 PUBLISHING
MARKHAM, ON
CANADA

Contents

Foreword

Take an ordinary spot in your neighborhood; a library or an intersection, and consider how you could gradually transform it into a hub of public activity. Add a few mobile tables and chairs outside the library, then a planter and a drinking fountain, and it changes the whole feel of the corner. A regular Saturday morning story time, along with a community message board in front and a playground for youngsters, turns the library into a community center. Then see what happens at either location when a coffee shop opens, some public art is created, and vendors arrive selling ice cream or garden produce. Done! You've got a great neighbourhood hangout for people from all cultures. A place you'll visit even when you're not looking for a book. You show up because you know something will be happening there.

As this book shows, it doesn't take much to bring life to neighbourhoods. Somehow in today's cosmopolitan cities we have lost the art of getting along. We live segregated lives. I share a neighbourhood with people from different parts of the world, but to what extent do I actually know them? I spend most of my time traveling or driving from one place to the next. There is nothing that motivates me to socialize with my neighbours. But what does that mean for the streets, parks, playgrounds, and other public spaces in the neighbourhood? Who goes there? Who uses them?

Bridging Cultures provides a step-by-step guide to bring people from diverse cultures together. Hanging out in your neighbourhood is the new lifestyle. It's good for health. It's good for business. It's good for creativity and innovation. It's good for a sense of belonging and community. Bridging Cultures shows the value of sociable public spaces. How places are planned and designed affects how we feel. The international case studies in this book provide ideas of social innovations that can turn your neighbourhood from conflict to peace, from indifference to activity. I will be using some of the ideas Noha has presented in this book to organize my own neighbourhood party!

In today's cosmopolitan world, Bridging Cultures is a breath of fresh air. At last there is a book that both ordinary citizens and civic leaders can use to optimize the creative and cultural benefits of social cohesion and to reinvigorate our public spaces. City Mayors, local authorities, housing associations, and developers are all going to want to get their hands on this book.

Raymond Aaron
New York Times Top Ten Best Selling Author

About the Author

Dr Noha Nasser is a passionate architect, urban designer, academic and consultant who believes that community-based solutions to urban design can build a strong identity of place and bring people together. Noha is an award-winning author and has published extensively on cultural diversity in areas of urban change where community cohesion makes social, cultural and economic sense. She runs a social enterprise called MELA where she works with a team of associates to deliver social innovations in public space to build social cohesion. Noha has been actively involved in testing creative ways to engage with different cultures that dispel myths, build a sense of community, and co-design public spaces to meet people's needs.

www.melasocialenterprise.com

Acknowledgements

I would like to thank a number of people who have been instrumental in the writing of this book. Mashuq Ally, Head of Equality and Diversity, Birmingham City Council gave of his time to share with me Birmingham's social cohesion challenges. I value your wisdom and hope this book provides some solutions to the on-going challenges. I would also like to thank Jas Bains, CEO of Ashram Moseley Housing Association for our inspiring conversations about social innovation. I really understand your commitment to people living peaceful lives with others. This book was inspired by some of your projects. I am indebted to Phil Wood for his listening ear, ready advice, and great book on Intercultural Cities from which I drew inspiration. I hope you find this book on public space a useful handbook. I want to also acknowledge Martin Field for his belief in the value of this book in relation to competitive cities, and to people doing things for themselves. As a developer this is rare to find!

My final thanks go to a number of people in my life. Thank you to Lucinda Offer for inviting me to spend time in her beautiful home to write peacefully. Thank you to my parents for their on-going support and belief in getting my message out. Thank you to my sister for providing light relief. I also thank Silas Lees for holding me to account. I dedicate this book to my children, Suzy and Sherief, for their love and unwavering support for my contribution to the world.

PART ONE

Chapter 1
Why Bridging Cultures Matters

"Cities have the capability of providing something for everybody, only because, and only when, they are created by everybody."
Jane Jacobs

Introduction

Visiting a city like London, Paris, Amsterdam, New York or Sydney, it's not long before you get a sense of the impact of the movement of people from one part of the world to the other. Often people are seeking better jobs, quality of life, business opportunities, and personal safety. For me, a second generation female migrant from Egypt who has grown up in London and lived in Egypt, Saudi Arabia, Japan, and now lives back in London, I have always been fascinated by how it has been possible to adapt to these different cultural contexts and make new friends.

I consider myself a true cosmopolitan; a citizen of the world. I have always wondered whether my ability to 'mingle' and 'get along with the locals' had something to do with my attitude towards others. Was it my willingness to reach out and bridge the cultural divide? When I look back at how those interactions with people occurred, I realise there were 'circumstances'; points of contact with people who later became my friends.

In London, as I grew up in the 1970s, it was the classroom and the playground where new relationships were forged. Joint school projects, after school clubs and playing group games were opportunities. In my teenage years growing up in Egypt, new relationships were made in the Sporting Club and the University. One person would introduce me to another, followed by an invitation to join a group. Even within the potentially challenging social context of Saudi Arabia, my friendship network was created in the workplace. The local girls' school where I taught English is where I met other teachers. My access to friends in Japan was again through teaching English in several schools. My husband's social networks at his workplace, and organised events by the YWCA helped foster cross-cultural understanding.

In conclusion, two fundamental ingredients are required for new friendships and social interactions to happen between cultures. The first ingredient is down to the individual and their mindset. They have to be willing to engage with people from different cultural backgrounds. This mindset is what I call the 'myths and stories' we learn about other people - our prejudices - our own cultural stories about others that are picked up from our parents, society and through film, news or social media. Ideas shape our opinions. The important point, is that prejudice is learned. We can unlearn prejudice when we connect on a much deeper level; when the focus is on what we have in common. The second ingredient is the 'circumstances' in which meaningful social interactions occur. These lead to lasting relationships. As in my personal story, there were particular spaces and social networks that 'enabled' a meaningful encounter. They were characterised by a shared interest or a common friend.

It is these two ingredients of dispelling 'myths and stories' and creating 'circumstance' in public spaces that I believe are the basis of social innovations for bridging cultures. Playgrounds, schools, and public events are meeting places. What this book explores are different scenarios where these two ingredients are present. Real case studies show that public spaces have these ingredients. This book is also interested in measurable improvement in the level of cross-cultural understanding, and opportunities for new relationships. As an urban designer and social entrepreneur, I am passionate about people having a strong shared sense of belonging to their local area. Places that have respect and peace between people of different cultures. The aim of this book is to inspire you in finding new and creative ways to bridge cultures in your cosmopolitan cities. I have taken the ideas in this book as the foundation of my social enterprise, MELA. MELA aims to transform people's 'myths and stories'. We aim to create social encounters that build a sense of community. We are passionate about generating new and creative ideas about public spaces with local people. This book is at the source of MELA's commitment for peaceful and convivial neighbourhoods.

The Competitive Advantage of Cultural Diversity

The concept of 'bridging social capital' was first introduced by Robert Putnam in his article 'Bowling Alone: America's Declining Social Capital'. The article highlighted the declining numbers of voters, the emptying out of bowling alleys and other social meeting places for lack of patrons, and the loss of a sense of community ties. Putnam defined this decline of civic engagement in the idea of 'social capital'. Social capital is the value placed on social networks and ties that affect economic productivity, happiness, health, crime levels, and open democracy. He explained that social capital refers to the connections among individuals based on mutual support, cooperation, and trust.

Putnam also distinguished between two forms of social capital; bonding and bridging. In the case of bonding social capital, people relate to others who reinforce similar cultural identities. They risk becoming inward-looking as a way to build solidarity and self-help. In the case of bridging social capital, however, social networks are outward-facing. They encompass people across diverse social groupings. Although there are pros and cons for both forms of social capital, and many people combine both forms, this book is particularly interested in bridging social capital. Bridging capital are linkages to external networks that broaden social circles and allow for greater innovation and economic success.

The trend that Putnam's article highlighted was the extent in which people were withdrawing from their communities. One measure of this decline was the loss of trust in strangers. In America in the 1960s, Putnam reported that more than half of all Americans said they trusted others. Today fewer than a third say the same thing. Similarly in the UK in the 1950s, more than two-thirds of British people said that most people could be trusted. In the 1990s that had fallen to 29 per cent of the population. Sociologists blame the decline of what they call 'traditional trust' to increased choice, diversity and mobility. Without traditional trust there is an increase in social isolation, and a decline in close friendships.

This lack of trust and social connections has a cost. According to the UK's independent Social Integration Commission, the drop in social mobility and increased isolation between groups means that problems are emerging in areas from employment to health. This costs the UK the equivalent of 0.5 per cent of GDP or £6bn each year. The impact alone on the long-term jobless, whose lack of contact with those in work means they are likely to remain unemployed for longer, is estimated to be £1.5bn. At a community level, factors such as a lack of friendships across age groups are resulting in loneliness and anxiety. The associated costs are £700m in healthcare and £1.2bn for treating an increased prevalence of cardiovascular disease.

The economic case for greater social capital is not just about prevention and addressing the deficit. In fact there are many economists who consider the benefits of social capital from the perspective of co-operation, trust and coordinated action between trading individuals and companies. Increased social capital maximises economic interests whilst at the same time maximizing social welfare.

Several commentators have also drawn on the economic growth resulting from bridging social capital. One commentator, Richard Florida, with his creative capital theory, states that those cities most open to diversity of all sorts and with high densities of culturally diverse populations are what promote innovation and economic growth. Diversity gives them their competitive edge. Phil Wood and Charles Landry, call intercultural innovation, the 'diversity advantage' in which bridging social capital supports:

- Business start-ups and competitiveness
- Workforce diversity and competitiveness
- Linguistic diversity and competitiveness
- Cultural diversity, creativity and competitiveness
- Supplier diversity and competitiveness
- Diaspora and international networks and competitiveness

In fact, The London Development Agency promotes diversity as one of London's greatest strengths. £90 billion sales were recorded for Black Asian Minority ethnic owned businesses in 2004. Wood and Landry argue that cross-cultural interactions have been a major source of new ideas and innovations. In their interviews of leading migrant entrepreneurs in London they conclude: 'each of these entrepreneurs borrows some aspects from their original culture and applies it to the identification of new niches where they can innovate and leave their mark. Each builds on the social, economic and cultural strengths of their original community, but then departs from it and creates something that at times is alien, or in conflict with their community. However, it is precisely this tension and this need to break with tradition that gives them strength and the impetus to expand into new ventures. It is usually at this stage that they seek like-minded people to work with. And this is also why they prefer to employ people from diverse backgrounds, rather than from their own. It is the talent, the flexibility and the capacity to adapt that they seek in colleagues and employees from other backgrounds and not the security of family ties, or the cultural understanding of the ethnic group.

Healthy Happy Diverse Neighbourhoods

The relationship between people from different cultures trusting each other and co-operating has a positive health impact. Strong networks, good levels of support and positive relationships help integrate individuals and communities. They are important factors for good health and well-being. The benefits of increased bridging social capital include increased confidence and self-esteem. A sense of connectedness and belonging, and the ability to bring about change in a person's own life or in the community, all contribute.

In a study by the Young Foundation, they found that neighbourliness is a crucial factor in creating a shared sense of belonging. The study defines neighbourliness as 'the observable social interaction and exchange of help and goods'. In neighbourhoods where there is a high concentration of one cultural group, the study warns neighbourliness can lead to segregation. The study offers four factors to encourage neighbourliness. The first factor is that neighbourliness improves well-being and happiness when there is a shared sense of belonging in the community. The second is that neighbourliness facilitates mutual aid and support between people through daily social interactions. Interactions help build a comfortable atmosphere of substantial relationships and emotional support. The third factor is informal social control and cutting crime. More neighbours knowing each other and looking out for each other creates an atmosphere of safety. And lastly, the fourth factor is improving life chances. Children growing up in neighbourhoods with high levels of trust and strong local networks can significantly help with career progression and employment. Having the right kind of contacts for various purposes that provides access to new information and resources, enhances people's ability to solve their problems. In relation to health issues, bridging capital has been proven to facilitate faster and wider diffusion of information. In turn this promotes healthier behaviours and controls unhealthy behaviours.

There are many benefits to health and well-being that bridging social capital provides in diverse neighbourhoods. The challenge remains in building bridges between cultures. In research by the UK Home Office, it is not surprising that more ethnically diverse areas have lower levels of trust. Similarly, the Commission for Racial Equality found that people are happier with people like themselves. In a World Bank study on the different relationship between bonding and bridging social capital on individual life satisfaction they found that those with more balanced attitudes towards family and friends and towards work and leisure are happier. What remains a determining factor in the levels of well-being and life satisfaction, as well as the degree of bridging capital in areas that are culturally diverse, is deprivation. It is this topic that requires some discussion.

The Spatial Geography of Social Inequality

The benefits of bonding capital to provide solidarity, greater levels of trust, and emotional support are well known. There are disadvantages, however, when cultural groups become inward-looking and spatially segregated. There is a great deal of research on the unequal spatial and economic distribution of cultural groups in so-called 'ghettoes' and 'ethnic enclaves' in the city.

Some commentators focus on these spatial concentrations as self-defined territories. They protect and enhance a cultural group's economic, social and cultural development. Particular cases are representative of this type of spatial concentration. Culture is used as a commodity to attract business and people. Places like Chinatowns worldwide, Brick Lane in East London, The Golden Mile in Manchester and The Balti Triangle in Birmingham are commodified. They have developed their brand from the Place's predominant cultural identity. In many cases, the way in which culture is symbolised undermines the authenticity of the predominant culture. It is modified in ways that is 'acceptable' and 'palatable' to the wider public. Those in favour of this type of enclave, argue that migrants are successfully creating an economic niche to enhance their status and maintain their cultures. At the same time, the attraction of these enclaves to the wider public enhances familiarity and greater tolerance.

Those not in favour of spatial cultural concentrations consider that cultural groups are forced to surrender their authentic cultural identity as means of acceptance into the mainstream. In effect, they are being required to change their cultural identity to fit in. The wider society is attracted to these places for 'the exotic experience'. There is little interest in socially and culturally engaging with these cultures. Whilst these ethnic enclaves may be successful in their own right, they perpetuate the separation between groups. Richard Sennett so aptly describes this 'dissociation as a version of civility. Fragmentation as a form of freedom. A social compromise which works against shared citizenship'.

In contrast to these ethnic economic spatial concentrations, more deprived spatial concentrations have been commonly called ghettoes. The term has a historical association with distinctly separate Jewish neighbourhoods. The ghettoes were closed off from the remainder of the city during the night. It was a means of forced physical, cultural and economic separation. The term is popular in Chicago's School of Sociology urban ecology mode. Neighbourhoods in the city are identified as natural arrival points for migrants. In some cases migrants became trapped in these areas. In other cases, over a period of time, migrants begin to disperse and assimilate into more cosmopolitan neighbourhoods in the wider city. What later emerged was that many of the ghettoes and slums identified by the urban ecology model were racially institutionalised spatial discrimination. This took the form of housing policy and 'red lining'. It prevented mobility from one neighbourhood to another. This form of social engineering was common in the US and the UK. Cultural mobility was constrained through controls in property deeds.

More recently, since the 1980s with the rise of new liberal capitalism and increased globalisation, the privatisation of large tracts of land for urban regeneration has led to a new form of spatial inequality. Urban developers have built housing for the new wealthy and mobile creative classes. Concentrated pockets in city centres, along revived canal sides and in new suburbs on the edge of cities. Many of these new housing developments are protected by gates and CCTV cameras. They enclose themselves in 'enclaves for the rich'. In her book *Ground Control*, Anna

Minton, describes these prison-like outposts of the rich. They are obsessed with security. She argues that the obsession with eliminating chance through heavy surveillance helps create insidious fear. She notes that the fear of crime rising is in direct correlation with a fall in the crime rate.

At the same time, the enclaves of the poor are being issued with antisocial behaviour orders. In these neighbourhoods poverty is criminalised. They become a social problem. A pervasive threat to the moral order and the social cohesion of cities. The assumption is that deprived neighbourhoods lack the necessary ingredients which foster social cohesion. However, there is evidence to the contrary.

In the report on 'Our Shared Future' by the Commission on Integration and Cohesion, several factors that influence social cohesion in neighbourhoods were identified. Deprivation remains a key influencer. The fact that some areas with high deprivation also have high cohesion shows that local action can build resilience to its effects. Other influencers include crime and anti-social behaviour, discrimination, diversity, immigration and the unfair allocation of resources. The international connections in places add complexity. Overall, the report found a pattern as neighbourhoods become increasingly diverse. Initially there are tensions, then adaptation, increasing acceptance and finally positive espousal of diversity. Based on these complex influencers and patterns, the report introduces integration and cohesion as two interlinked processes; 'cohesion is principally the process that must happen in all communities to ensure different groups of people get on well together; and integration is principally the process that ensures new residents and existing residents adapt to one another'. In their new definition of a cohesive community they state:

- There is a common vision and a sense of belonging for all communities
- The diversity of people's backgrounds and circumstances are appreciated and positively valued
- Those from different backgrounds have similar life opportunities
- Strong and positive relationships are being developed between people from different backgrounds in the workplace, in schools, and within neighbourhoods

Many of these characteristics of a cohesive community can be fostered at the scale of the neighbourhood and the public spaces that bring people together in cosmopolitan cities. The next section considers the qualities of a cosmopolitan city where societies are cohesive. There is also a socio-economic and spatial equality between different cultural groups.

The Cosmopolitan City

The concept of the 'Cosmopolis' is one in which cultural diversity is embraced as a force for good; socially, politically, economically, and in the built and open spaces of the city. There is a great deal of evidence supporting the negative effects of social, economic and cultural polarization. Uneven distribution of power between different cultural groups in the city to access resources and assets is common. Cosmopolis, however, is a goal for social and spatial justice. It is the ongoing process towards a socially cohesive city. It is the city, and its neighbourhoods, where people from different cultural backgrounds live their everyday lives. Where they make claims to their rights to the city and its spaces, as citizens. For the purposes of this book, citizenship and the practice of open democracy is an important and fundamental factor. For a truly democratic city, its citizens, no matter what their cultural backgrounds should feel they belong. Their histories are recognized and their cultural demands are respected and met. According to the philosopher Iris Marion Young, she states: 'In the ideal of city life, freedom leads to group differentiation; to the formation of affinity groups, but this social and spatial differentiation of groups is without exclusion. . . . The interfusion of groups in the city occurs partly because of the multiuse differentiation of social space. What makes urban spaces interesting, draws people out in public to them, gives people pleasure and excitement, is the diversity of activities they support.'

The case for diversity is strong; mixing cultural groups is the ultimate basis of a better and more attractive place. It fosters creativity, it encourages tolerance, and it leads to city officials appreciating the cross-fertilization potential of different lifestyles. Innovative economic opportunities arise. The engineering of social mixing is not a new concept. In the 19th century, idealists like The Settlement Houses and Co-Partnerships of Samuel and Henrietta Barnett, Octavia Hill, Jane Addams and others were aimed at educating and socializing the poor. They also sensitised the rich through deliberate social mix in urban places. In planning history, the utopian communities of the Garden City Movement at the turn of the twentieth century sought to house different social groups in varying degrees of physical closeness and encouraged the use of shared community facilities. What Garden City neighbourhoods demonstrated was communities can be bound together with strong shared moral and social values. The predominantly Quaker principles for social justice was the basis for these values. These values were important a hundred years ago when mainly social and economic class disparities existed. Today, however, cultural diversity adds a further level of complexity in relation to values. In fact, some critics argue that diversity and tolerance of the 'Other' is challenging in contexts where lifestyles are incompatible or irreconcilable. In this case, it is not group identities but a collective identity that should prevail. I don't disagree, however, I assert that collective identity needs to be robust enough to allow for socialization process in which everyday contact and tolerance can be learned.

The neighbourhood as a physical boundary is the arena where tolerance can be learned. A series of overlapping social networks in which the quality and strength of ties between neighbours is a measure. Several studies have shown the importance of unpretentious everyday casual social contact, or 'weak ties', that happen in neighbourhoods. They are a source of feeling at home, security, and practical as well as social support. The theory of weak ties suggests that acquaintances generated by such everyday interactions like borrowing tools or simply a casual hello in the street, lead to people being better connected to the wider world. Weak ties also are more likely to provide people with information about ideas, threats and opportunities stimulating creativity and innovation. Therefore, the differences between neighbourhoods is best understood as the differences between the form and content of social networks, the quality and frequency of weak ties, that arguably are the building blocks of social cohesion. Access to learning tolerance, co-operation, and a sense of belonging is fundamental.

The aim of this book is to provide the key values that will support people in learning to live together regardless of their cultural background, inspired by what we have in common rather than what divides us. It is a society based on solidarity and a common vision for equality for all sections of the community. Interaction between different cultural groups and participation by all sections of the community in civic engagement. Key to civic engagement and participation is the role of shared spaces to re-build strong community ties and networks of social support and reciprocity. Hence the focus of this book is to demonstrate how social networks can be strengthened in the use and re-use of public spaces. The factors that support people of different cultural backgrounds to participate, engage and interact with others . Fundamentally, it is about the practices and processes of social innovation that bring people together to do things together. The next section will explain what social innovation is and why it is important in bridging cultures.

Social Innovation: the way forward

In meeting the needs of an equitable cosmopolitan city, this book examines the ideas people have created to encourage bridging capital. How is it used to resolve conflicts and segregation between people of different cultural backgrounds? These ideas are called social innovations because they are products, services and models that address pressing unmet needs to improve people's lives. They provide the solutions to social cohesion. Cultivating social innovation starts from the presumption that people are competent interpreters of their own lives and competent solvers of their own problems. The case studies that follow in this book are based on social innovations in public space that address the needs of local people where neither the market nor the state has adequately met their needs. Innovations will have led to new or improved capabilities and relationships and better use of assets and resources. In other words, social innovations are both good for society and enhance society's capacity to act.

The case studies in this book are founded on innovators' understanding of people's needs and dislocations, dissatisfactions and blockages. As an example, Michael Young, the founder of the Young Foundation for social innovation got many of his best ideas from random conversations on street corners, buses and even in cemeteries. Similarly in 1864, when Ruskin bought three buildings in Paradise Place, a notorious slum, and gave them to Octavia Hill to manage, the aim was to make 'lives noble, homes happy, and family life good'. Her determination, personality, and skill transformed the poverty-stricken areas into tolerably harmonious communities by providing communal amenities such as meeting halls, savings clubs, and dramatic productions. Her training programmes laid the foundations of the modern profession of housing management and her first organisation, the Horace Street Trust (now Octavia Housing and Care) became the model for all subsequent housing associations.

The drivers of social innovation tend to be based on a sharp external push that galvanises the will to change. This is accompanied by the subsequent emergence of a strong internal capacity to develop innovations. To put innovations into practice what is required is the right leadership, structures and organisational culture. To embed the social innovation, a critical factor is mobilising the right external resources by galvanising stakeholder support, partnerships and funding and mobilising a set of networks to embed change.

As in the examples of Michael Young and Octavia Hill, two factors underpin successful social innovation; the first factor is the vision of local leaders' and the participation of citizens in meeting this vision. Several commentators call these key individuals 'social actors', 'social entrepreneurs' and 'local heroes' in the development of social innovation. In many cases, social innovation arises from a crisis or a pressing social demand or challenge within which leadership emerges.

According to a report by NESTA, it is more likely leadership emerges from the public, voluntary and third sector, and less likely from local citizens. However, with the current policy context for greater devolution and the UK's recent 'Big Society' values, greater emphasis is being placed on reviving and enabling local democracy. Citizens are being encouraged to contribute and shape new ideas themselves. According to the European Commission research mapping citizen engagement in social innovation in Europe, the typology for mapping citizen engagement in the production of the social innovation process is four fold:

- Understanding individual needs and problems: in this case citizens provide information and resources to shape the ideas based on their own experience
- Understanding larger patterns and trends: in this case citizens provide widely accessible platforms to crowdsource data, nowadays many of these platforms are digital and act as open-source innovation platforms for ideas to be shared between amateurs, experts, professionals, funders and other stakeholders
- Co-developing solutions: is a case where citizens are problem-solving through a creative approach of collaborating with service providers to develop solutions together. It may also include co-operative governance in re-distributing power and influencing the delivery of services.
- Crowdsourcing solutions: in this case opens up a function performed by an organisation to a wider number of people to undertake the function collaboratively. A key feature of this new model of production and problem solving is it is open, online and distributed leading to mining the crowd for information and solutions.

The report highlights the benefits of citizen engagement in social innovation: 'We have argued in this paper and elsewhere that there are reasons why citizen engagement may be of particular importance to social innovation: first, citizens have specific knowledge of their own lives which no organisation can claim; engagement processes therefore enable a better understanding of problems that an innovation might address.

Second, citizens can be the source of innovative ideas. Third, engaging citizens enables contributions from varied and sometimes unexpected sources, which introduces divergent thinking; these diverse perspectives add particular value when trying to address complex challenges. Fourth, innovations which are developed by and with citizens may be seen as more legitimate than those which are developed without engagement activities. And finally, many of the challenges that social innovations aim to tackle, such as obesity or climate change, absolutely require the participation, co-operation and 'buy-in' of citizens because they depend on fundamental changes to behaviour and attitudes.'

The second factor is how social innovation is adopted, scaled up and disseminated. The NESTA report identifies five stages in the social innovation lifecycle:

- The first phase is the critical issue that triggers the need for social innovation
- The second phase is the design and discover phase in which a variety of approaches are developed
- The third phase is the mobilisation of teams to pilot the approaches to innovation
- The fourth phase is mainstreaming the social innovation so that it grows in scale and becomes routine in processes and practices
- The final phase is embedding where the social innovation gets disseminated to other fields and sectors thanks to inspiration or infection.

Some of the case studies in this book may not have completed the entire social innovation cycle, yet they hold within them the potential to change behaviours and attitudes towards other people of different cultures and towards the engagement with public space.

CHECKLIST

- Have you mapped the neighbourhood in relation to bonding and bridging capital?
- Have you mapped the neighbourhood in relation to levels of trust, co-operation and collaboration in the context of happiness, life satisfaction, mental health and well-being?
- Have you mapped the neighbourhood in relation to the 'diversity advantage' (business start-ups, workforce diversity, linguistic diversity, cultural diversity, creativity, supplier diversity and extent of international networks)?
- Have you mapped the degree of social, economic and spatial segregation (ethnic enclaves, ghettoes, and gated communities)?
- Have you mapped the level of social cohesion in relation to deprivation, crime and anti-social behaviour, discrimination, diversity, immigration and the unfair allocation of resources?
- Have you mapped the quality and frequency of weak ties?
- Have you mapped the degree of physical closeness of different residential layouts housing different social groups, and the use of shared community facilities?
- Have you mapped any social innovation products, service and models that meet social needs, have clear leaders in the community, and organizational culture to support social innovation with access to wider stakeholder support?

- Have you mapped the level of citizen engagement in the products, services and models of social innovation in the neighbourhood that can be enhanced or encouraged?

Chapter 2
Why Public Space?

"...that the sight of people attracts still other people, is something that city planners and city architectural designers seem to find incomprehensible. They operate on the premise that city people seek the sight of emptiness, obvious order and quiet. Nothing could be less true. The presences of great numbers of people gathered together in cities should not only be frankly accepted as a physical fact – they should also be enjoyed as an asset and their presence celebrated."
Jane Jacobs

Public Space as a Social Arena

Public spaces are a fundamental feature of cities and urban culture. In cities around the world, urban spaces such as plazas, markets, streets, town halls temples and urban parks have long been centres of civic life where people encounter each other, socialize, exchange goods and have face-to-face interactions. In these key public spaces there are opportunities for gathering, recreation, festivals, and trading as well as protests and demonstrations. The quality, functionality and accessibility of public spaces in a city are commonly perceived to be a measure of the quality of urban life. They can be both outdoor and indoor. Civic buildings are also key public spaces because it is in these internal spaces where the community meets, socialises and shares experiences, making the buildings a part of the public realm. Key public spaces are therefore at the heart of bridging cultures as an arena for cross-cultural mixing and shared understanding. They are the vital arena for differences to be encountered and negotiated. The value of public space is in the everyday sociability that takes place. They are the spaces in which we can learn to live with others through seeing different norms and ways of behaving.

An important and commonly held view of what makes good public spaces is the degree of accessibility and freedom of expression that truly democratic, open and inclusive public spaces provide. From the days of the Greek Agora, the democratic nature of public space has shaped society and has been the site for the conduction of politics. Commonly perceived as the unit of measure for assessing the health of our democracy, it is in public spaces that we negotiate our common interests and express our differences, where we celebrate creativity and display our dissent. The term 'public space' refers to a place that is open and accessible to everyone, regardless of gender, culture, or socio-economic background.

There is no single definition of inclusive public space; however, commentators define four dimensions of accessibility:

- Physical access allows people to be physically present with no barriers to getting in to the space and moving in and through it regardless of age and ability
- Social access (or 'symbolic access') involves the presence of cues, in the form of people, design and management elements, suggesting who is and who is not welcome in the space
- 'Visual access' or 'visibility' of public spaces use symbols, or landmarks, within these spaces and provide a feeling of safety and comfort, as well as belonging
- Access to activities where public space provides a diverse and multifunctional range of activities that meets the needs of diverse cultures, genders, abilities and ages

More accessible public spaces promote sociability and the 'circumstances' for social encounters that bridge between cultures. The well-established Project for Public Spaces (PPS) describes good places as places that offer people many different reasons to go there. They are places where we want to 'hangout' for some time because the place offers us a variety of activities, experiences, and comfort. These places are clearly identifiable from a distance, easy to enter when you get closer, and simple to use. Taking this idea of 'hangouts' one step further, Ray Oldenburg, in his seminal book *The Great Good Place: cafes, coffee shops, bookstores, bars, hair salons and other hangouts at the heart of the community*, defines the core qualities of those 'hangouts'. He calls them 'third spaces', or public spaces that host the regular, voluntary, informal and happily anticipated gatherings of individuals beyond the realms of home and work. He describes their qualities as:

- Being 'neutral ground', where individuals can come and go as they please
- Being highly inclusive, accessible and without formal criteria of membership
- Their 'taken-for-granted-ness' and low profile
- Being open during and outside office hours
- Being characterised by a 'playful mood'
- Providing psychological comfort and support
- With conversation their 'cardinal and sustaining' activity, providing 'political fora of great importance'

These are the types of spaces where people can enjoy the social vibrancy of urban life and seeing other people. They can also be places of retreat and relief from dense urban districts and structured everyday life. Places of retreat, such as parks, a cemetery, or footpaths that are close to water, provided opportunities for reflection. Markets and neighbourhood spaces provide the spaces for meeting friends and support networks.

Both types of third places support well-being and have therapeutic functions.

But public spaces are more than just containers of human activity. They are also collective expressions of a city, as well as depositories of personal memories. Recollections of using a space when growing up, for example, could promote a sense of belonging, or prompt fond family memories. As places where important historical events tend to unfold, public spaces are imbued with important, collective meanings – both official and unofficial. People need a variety of public open spaces within a local area to meet a range of everyday needs: spaces to linger as well as spaces of transit; spaces that bring people together as well as spaces of retreat; green spaces as well as hard spaces such as streets or markets.

For Melissa Mean and Charlie Tims, authors of the report *People Make Places: Growing the Public Life of Cities,* public spaces act as self-organizing public services because they form 'a shared spatial resource from which experiences and value are created in ways that are not possible in our private lives alone.'

What this means is that public space is better understood not as a predetermined physical place, but as an experience created by the interaction between people and places. People need a variety of public spaces within a local area to meet. A range of places for everyday needs that reflect their lifestyle choices, value systems, and local traditions. These experiences together form the collective identity of a community. The report emphasises that the design of a public space to the highest standards providing top-quality facilities is not the most important factor in the creation of public space. In fact, it is the social benefits including the potential for well-being to be experienced that is ultimately the successful factor; it is what goes on within a space that is important. Here the value is placed on spaces that provide opportunities for different types of encounters – both casual and organised, routine or serendipitous. For Mean and Tims, they observe that public space in neighbourhoods, towns and cities is not in decline but is instead expanding. What they have found is that there are non-traditional spaces that create opportunities for association and exchange. Gatherings at the school gate, activities in community facilities, shopping malls, cafés and car boot sales are some non-traditional spaces. Mean and Tims re-define public space as any space where there are shared uses for a diverse range of activities by a range of different people regardless of appearance, or whether it is in public ownership.

In this book, public space provides the panacea for improved cross-cultural sociability. However, there are commentators who believe we are asking too much of public space. Richard Sennett, for example, discerns three dominant modes in which different groups live together, each of which is deficient: conflict, assimilation and indifference. He argues that in present day cities we are sliding towards indifference as a way to cope with the presence of 'others' where public spaces might be shared by groups. They don't really bring people together. He observes that public spaces are increasingly segmented spaces. They are based on self-selection and focusing on a narrow range of activities. At the same time there are concerns that open and uncontrolled public spaces, sites of 'unpredictable encounter', have been increasingly privatised. Public spaces have become subject to controls and surveillance, particularly in a post 9/11 world and the post-riots context. Some question the desire to live together in the first place and oppose the 'thrown togetherness' that characterizes cosmopolitan cities. As Jane Jacobs points out: 'Cities are full of people with whom, from your viewpoint, or mine, or any other individual's, a certain degree of contact is useful or enjoyable; but you do not want them in your hair.' The challenge is how to encourage sociability whilst maintaining privacy and anonymity. Are there ways in which diverse neighbourhoods can create a shared sense of place where proximity can be negotiated? The next section considers the factors that create a sense of belonging.

Identity and Place-Attachment

When arriving and settling in a new place for the first time, neighbourliness becomes a crucial factor in creating a shared sense of belonging. The Young Foundation has done some work on 'neighbourliness'. It is a way to negotiate the choices people have in helping their neighbours during time of great need, but at the same time respecting boundaries which allow people to retain their sense of privacy. Respecting boundaries is articulated as a key aspect of good neighbourliness. The Foundation identified two types of neighbourliness; 'manifest neighbourliness' defined as the observable social interaction and exchange of help and goods; and 'latent neighbourliness' defined as the feelings or inclination towards neighbourliness which turns into actions during times of great need. In their view, latent neighbourliness is more appropriate in the modern world where society is focused on the individual. Closely connected with neighbourliness is sense of belonging, however, the Foundation argues that a sense of belonging to a neighbourhood does not necessarily lead to neighbourly behaviour and increased civic engagement. At the same time, a lack of belonging and feelings of isolation do not necessarily lead to anti-social behaviour. Nonetheless, people can instinctively sense acceptance from groups such as family, colleagues, the neighbourhood and society.

The public realm also plays an important role to support neighbourliness. For example, real or perceived levels of safety will have an impact, as do poorly designed and maintained public spaces. The key is that public spaces need to function as places that encourage social interaction, create memories and meaning, and are welcoming and safe.

In spatial terms, sense of place, or the meanings and attachment to a place held by the collective in defining its identity, has been commonly referred to as place attachment. It combines the physical setting, human activities, and human social and psychological processes associated with the setting. A place is a centre of meaning based on human experience, social relationships, emotions, and thoughts. According to Tuan the sense of place is based on the length and depth of experience within the place, whereas Relph argues social relationships in the place is the basis of attachment rather than the physical landscape itself. Therefore, place attachment is the nature of the bond between people and the place where they settle. For new settlers, these bonds take time and are built through extensive interaction with a place. People may begin to define themselves in terms of that place. They cannot really express who they are without inevitably taking into account the setting that surrounds them.

For groups from different cultural backgrounds, their identity is closely associated with a psychological attachment to familiar symbols. Spatial features are important, such as a temple or uses of the space such as cultural celebrations. The question, is how can a collective identity be created where there are diverse cultures?

Some commentators argue that a communal identity can only be created when there is an overarching collective identity. Collective identity nurtures diversity but does not privilege difference. In other words, an approach that encompasses a set of values rather than giving primacy to a single value . Collective identity develops through a shared experience, a common culture, or lifestyle. All places are imbued with multiple meanings. Lynch noted that the identity of a place distinguishes it from other places but that this identity may vary between people. Some suggest individualistic place meanings; a given place will contain as many different meanings as there are people using the place. This suggests that inclusive place identities will accommodate multiple identities without singling one out, and become accessible to all social groups. There is often a symbiotic relationship between people's attachments to their area and their experience of public spaces.

Places like markets tend to attract people from all backgrounds because they offer opportunities for casual social encounters, lingering, and buying.

For many people, local social networks are a principal source of attachment to place. Other factors such as continuity in place and people's perception and response to demographic and physical changes in their neighbourhood also lead to place attachment. A strong sense of belonging is created by use of local facilities and distinctiveness. Layouts of housing, the nearby presence of public buildings or the cultural diversity of the area could distinguish, either favourably or unfavourably, the area from other places.

The big question is how to begin creating a strong sense of belonging and place attachment? What process can be used to build places where people want to hang out? PPS suggest implementing bottom-up strategies that recognise citizens as the experts. They believe places guided by the wisdom of the community build a strong partnership between the public, private and third sectors. PPS identify a number of key actions to foster a sense of shared community:

- Create places where people can stop to sit and chat with each other, such as putting a bench out in front of your house
- Tame traffic in neighborhoods by making streets so interesting that people naturally slow down to see what is going on.
- Develop new activities for teens that make them want to get involved in the future of their neighborhood instead of feeling excluded and alienated from the community.
- Introduce new kinds of park activities, such as gardens catering to certain groups — for example, children, seniors, or various ethnic groups — or a bread oven that is used to cook community dinners.
- Improve safety and security in a neighborhood by encouraging people to do things like saying hello to everyone they see. This can change the spirit of a community faster and more effectively than a police presence will ever do.
- Bring new kinds of people to the local neighbourhood centre with creative campaigns that deliver social and economic benefits for the place.
- Promote new opportunities for social interaction and community pride by introducing activities from different cultures, such as bocce ball courts, casitas, or an evening promenade.
- Make kids healthier by developing innovative programs so they can safely walk or bike to school.
- Establish more effective community-based planning processes that result in less arguing, more public input, and a general level of agreement on what to do to make the community better.
- Foster new types of businesses that not only make money but also have more far reaching impacts — for example, rent fun and unique bikes to people who don't ordinarily ride bikes, like seniors, disabled people, and young children.

- Champion your local hangout by making it a 'Third Place' such as a coffee shop, café or other spot where everyone feels welcome and can strike up a conversation with their neighbours.
- Provide clean public restrooms through enterprising programs that grow out of partnerships between businesses and the neighbourhood association.

Circumstances for Social Interaction

At the start of this book, I described two factors that gave me access to engaging with different cultural contexts and creating 'bridging' social networks. The first was a mindset which will be discussed in the following chapter, and the second was the circumstances in which social interaction took place. I identified certain key public spaces where opportunities for interaction were present, what I called circumstances. These circumstances were of two types. The first was the nature of the public space and the second was the presence of peers that invited me in to a social network. This section looks at the qualities of these public spaces that support social interaction. In the previous section, we established that public space is increasingly being considered in terms of its sociability capacity rather than its physical properties.

Two general types of social interaction in public open spaces can be identified: casual social encounters, such as chance meetings on a street, and organised social events and activities, for instance, a carnival in a park. The opportunity for informal interaction, or weak ties, is one of the most valued aspects of public open spaces. Casual encounters range from meetings with friends and neighbours in residential areas to brief exchanges with strangers in markets and shopping streets. But public space is not only for social interaction. It can also provide a place for relief, reflection, and retreat. Casual social interaction can itself be divided into two types: routine encounters and serendipitous encounters. Routine social encounters occur on a regular basis and are pre-arranged or occur in a set place and at a set time. These days many of these routine social encounters are arranged by technologically-enabled communication such as mobile phones, websites, social networking sites and Mobile Apps. However, sometimes routine encounters are both unorganised and unmediated while being more or less anticipated. These encounters often help to maintain loose ties between neighbours and familiar strangers but also provide the first step towards friendships. Routine meetings between people take place where people's everyday paths are most likely to cross: semi-domestic spaces (such as forecourts to flats and houses), residential streets, local shopping centres, the street outside a local mosque or a small park next to a primary school. One of the key qualities of these spaces is the opportunity and freedom to linger. Serendipitous encounters are the result of both regular and occasional use of spaces. Unexpected meetings are associated with particular spaces that enhance sociability. Places located outside the immediate neighbourhood arena that draw a greater number of people, such as a market or a main street, are more likely to be settings for serendipitous encounters.

There are a number of key circumstances that underpin successful socially-enabling public spaces; familiarity, proximity, regular use that meets everyday needs; endurance, freedom to linger, available facilities, and physical characteristics.

Casual encounters are more likely to occur in places that are familiar to people and where over time they can build trust. There are instances, however, where trust and familiarity can be fast-tracked when invitations by peers embed newcomers into existing social networks and encourage use. Familiarity is built up with routine visits to school, work, the market or the high street. They become familiar spaces of interaction where people come into contact with strangers regularly. Markets in particular provide an active and engaged community of traders that contribute to the social scene because of the opportunity for face-to-face conversations when selling goods.

Having public spaces in close proximity supports regular use. These public spaces can be quite non-descript, such as a telephone box or street railings, but they become a self-organised hang out. Street corners, forecourts and front gardens to houses, the pick-up area in front of a school within walking distance are all opportunities for people to venture out of their private spaces into the public realm.

The range and type of uses of public spaces that are adaptable to people's diverse and changing needs and desires is a significant factor. The study by Mean and Tims identified eight types of public space dictated by the activity happening within it at different times. The study was based on the central importance of trust and confidence from users in creating valuable public space. What they found was these spaces were not overly prescriptive in their design. They left room for self-organisation and encouraged a degree of appropriation. These 'spaces of potential' are:

- Exchange spaces: places where people exchange ideas, information and goods
- Productive spaces: used by people engaged in activities to grow or create goods
- Spaces of services provision: support services are run from these spaces, either by statutory or voluntary providers
- Activity spaces: where people gather for leisure, such as for play, sport or informal events

- Democratic / participative spaces: for shared decision-making or governance
- Staged spaces: 'one-off' special occasions where people are brought together for a specific purpose
- In-between spaces: places which are located between communities
- Virtual spaces: non-physical spaces, such as those created online by social networking sites

What these spaces provide are multiple uses, with different activities embedded or allowed throughout the day (such as e.g. shopping, commuting, play, the office lunch-hour, a café). They also hosted organised social activities such as public open-air events, football leagues, fairs or self-organised activities such as health walks, dog walking, picnics.

These uses also provide opportunities for social interaction or reflection. The public spaces may be vibrant and hard landscapes, or they may be quiet, private and green landscapes. What is fundamental is that they meet the needs of people at different stages in their lives and from different cultural contexts. For example, street markets are a valuable asset for many people and particularly the elderly in reducing isolation, and access to good, fresh and cheap food. It is spaces like these that move beyond mono-cultures and encourage diverse groups and activities to share common spaces.

The continuity of public spaces and their enduring nature is key to encounters with people. Regular encounters help build an individual sense of community. It is the basis for establishing closer ties.

The freedom to linger is another circumstance that provides impromptu and incidental encounters. People are allowed to remain in spaces without a specific reason. William H. Whyte in his seminal book, *The Social Life of Small Urban Spaces,* highlights the importance of seating in providing opportunities to 'watch the world go by' and for more meaningful encounters. Whyte explains the importance that seating be 'socially' comfortable; people have choice to sit alone, in groups, in the sun, in the shade, with their backs against something or not, etc. He also emphasises the importance of more impromptu sitting areas such as ledges and steps, as well as more formal benches and movable chairs.

Another circumstance for social interaction is what facilities are available that give purpose to a space and enhance its social vitality. A place that has one main purpose but can support many other diverse social activities facilitates encounters. As Whyte showed in his study of New York's plazas; adding seating, food, shops or toilets to a public space attracts people to that space and provides an opportunity to linger. As an example, a sports hall is a specific facility, however a small public space in front of it, a play ground nearby, and a café can provide opportunities for greater interactions either with people doing the same thing (e.g. ties between people on the same team sport) or people using the facility and its associated activities that are casual encounters.

The final circumstance for social interaction is how the design and layout of the physical space can encourage casual or serendipitous encounters. Jan Gehl, author of *Life Between Buildings,* draws correlations between the quality of the urban environment and the types of activities that take place. He found that 'necessary activities' that are more or less compulsory, such as going to school or work, took place no matter what the quality of the environment. 'Optional activities', however, such as taking a walk to get fresh air or sitting and sunbathing, only took place when the weather was favourable and conducive to this type of activity. On the other hand, he argues that 'resultant activities' or social activities, only take place in high quality public spaces that are designed to invite people to stop, sit, eat, play and so on. For example, a cul-de-sac or a homezone on a housing estate provides the opportunity for ball games and water fights among children and interaction between neighbours. We have already mentioned a number of key qualities for successful public spaces, however, there are key design features that affect the possibilities of meeting, seeing and hearing people.

- Accessible and easy to move through to anyone who desires access without barriers to any groups either physically or symbolically
- Legible in lay-out and design, with clear and recognisable routes, defined edges and clarity about the boundaries between public and private
- Distinctive, locally relevant, designed with local character and the community in mind through participation
- Open-ended, without exclusive domination of singular and incontestable cultural messages
- Safe and welcoming, give the idea of comfort and a degree of control, with for example good lighting and sightlines, and paying attention to different groups' needs with regard to safety
- Not over regulated but which rely on natural surveillance and active use for safety
- Features, such as a fountain, greenery or seating, that attract visitors to the place

Conflicts in Public Space

So far the focus of this chapter has been on how public spaces can provide opportunities for social encounters and cross-cultural exchanges. Yet we all know that public space is also contested. The recent London riots that spread nationwide in 2011 was a clear demonstration of angry youths taking to the streets to protest. On the news, we hear about gangs fighting over territories. Youths create social and economic solidarity in response to their marginal positions in society. In the post 9/11 world we are acutely aware of hyper security and surveillance. It limits our movement and freedom of self-expression. We also know that public space has increasingly excluded certain groups of people in society. Skateboarders, the homeless, poor people who can't afford the café culture, women, children, prostitutes are some of the excluded groups. Therefore contrary to popular belief that public space is democratic, open and inclusive, public space is also politically, socially and economically biased.

In many instances, public spaces are regulated by unofficial rules established by those in perceived power ('white' people in the case of the UK). The perceived superiority between different groups of people is at the root of many conflicts in public space. Racism and prejudice play a significant role in breaking down social interaction. They are based on myths and stories people have of others. The unconscious breaking of rules – the parking of a car in the wrong space, the inattentive disposal of rubbish, the lack of care for a front lawn – lead to people being ostracised or sometimes harassed. These unwritten rules and social norms not only serve to maintain a sense of order but are often used to legitimise prejudices against certain groups on cultural rather than racial grounds. For cultural minorities, public spaces can make them feel excluded because of additional deterrents created by unfamiliarity and fear of hostile or discriminatory behaviour. Such fears are corroborated and reflected in the 2003-04 crime figures which show, for example, that there were 4,179 prosecutions for racially aggravated crimes, of which 1,056 were assaults or harassment.

These types of conflicts tend to happen in the residential areas where there is a clearer distinction between 'insiders' and 'outsiders' than in places such as the general market where there is a greater sense of ownership over space. The perceived intrusion of outsiders could lead to tensions. In resolving issues of racism and prejudice, a raised awareness of different cultural norms and more open conversations are required.

Other forms of prejudice against young people is a recurring theme. Today, Anti-Social Behavior Orders against young people represent the mistrust adults have of young people 'hanging out'. With most young people spending their time in public space, this creates tensions. Some adults perceive large numbers of youths as a threat and avoid or tolerate them, whereas others take a more confrontational stance. The perception that young people are 'trouble makers' is largely down to the negative stereotyping that has defined neighbourhoods. The 'reputation effect' is exacerbated by the limited experience and mobility of people outside their own neighbourhoods. So while decrying some areas as being unsafe, external observers are projecting irrational opinions on neighbourhoods. These irrational 'beliefs' have proven to lower life chances. Many commentators point to the structural inequalities that face young people today as the root cause to much of the neighbourhood-based 'gang turfs'. In itself, turfs are not necessarily racially focused - often it is merely an expression of neighbourhood attachment taken to an extreme. To a degree, turfs should be recognised as an inherent aspect of young people's lives. It only becomes problematic in combination with other forms of deprivation and negative behaviour. Neighbourhood gangs as well as segregated communities are thus examples of the danger of 'bonding social capital' of the wrong kind. Too much belonging leads to the creation of clear turfs and psychological boundaries. In resolving conflicts, therefore, issues of inequality and marginalization require addressing.

To counter the preconceived opinion that is not based on reason or actual experiences between people of different races, cultures, genders, sexuality and generations, the need for openly talking about differences is required. This will open up a space for resolving conflicts. Greater cross-cultural understanding will result. It is also an opportunity to address some of the underlying structural issues that lead to conflict, many of which are related to economic marginalization and access to resources. It's a good place to start a conversation.

Spatially, access to housing, public space and community facilities are key urban resources. In many regeneration schemes and housing estate improvements, new development is inward-looking. Facilities are centrally located. Housing is separated according to socio-economic incomes. Richard Sennett describes the failure of a project in which he was involved in. He speaks about how 'boundary thinking can miss opportunities'. Tasked with the creation of a new market (La Marqueta) in Harlem, New York; 'we planners chose to locate La Marqueta in the centre of Spanish Harlem twenty blocks away, in the very centre of the community, and to regard 96th Street [where Harlem changes into a very wealthy area – the Upper East Side] as a dead edge, where nothing much happens. We chose wrongly. Had we located the market on that street, we might have encouraged activity which brought the rich and the poor into some daily commercial contact. Wiser planners have since learned from our mistake, and on the West Side of Manhattan sought to locate new community resources at the edges between communities, in order to open the gates between different racial and economic communities. Our imagination of the importance of the centre proved isolating, their understanding of the value of the edge and border has proved integrating.'

This is by no means easy. The problem with segregation and zoning is exactly its entrenchment and embedding in daily routines, as well as mental maps. Other examples include transport links that provided invaluable access for poorer residents on the outskirts of cities. Transport provides access to resources and services in the commercial centre. The point is that spatial layout and access to resources, such as public space, are fundamental to blurring the boundaries of inequality.

Social Cohesion and Public Space

In the previous section it was identified that negative perceptions of others, prejudice and racism break down social interaction in public space. In this section, the role of public space to bring about greater social cohesion is discussed. One commentator, Ash Amin, argues that public open spaces in cities are unlikely to encourage 'inter-ethnic understanding' because they are not 'spaces of inter-dependence and habitual engagement'. Rather, he suggests, people are more likely to come to terms with ethnic differences in places of more regular association such as the workplace, schools, youth centres and sports clubs 'where dialogue and 'prosaic negotiations' are compulsory'. Amin argues that it is the places in which we are obliged to be, combined with the opportunity or incentive for 'banal transgressions', which displace us from one cultural space into another, where new intercultural sociability is being formed.

Similarly, Stephen Vertovec emphasises the importance of such 'everyday practices for getting-on with others in the inherently fleeting encounters that comprise city life'. He uses the term 'civil-integration' in contrast to the 'deep and meaningful' encounters that he feels are unlikely to occur regularly in the context of super-diversity. Amin states that public space, in its widest sense, can be an operating mode for generating a kind of studied trust in urban multiplicity and public acceptance of 'throwntogetherness'. The acquiring and routinisation of civil-interaction to Vertovec includes 'simple forms of acknowledgement, acts of restricted helpfulness, types of personal consideration, courtesies, and 'indifference to diversity'. He argues, that these kinds of daily civility should be negotiated and promoted alongside wider ambitions for better relationships.

While relationships between community integration and public open spaces are not reducible to simple mechanisms, consideration of social processes is important. Intercultural understanding can illuminate the indirect role played by such spaces. Positive perceptions of public spaces such as shopping streets contribute to people's decisions to stay in the area. Long-term residence and regular interaction in neighbourhood spaces have a positive influence on intercultural relations; attitudes to difference among varied groups of neighbours is improved. Therefore, the continuity of social relations over time, and the endurance of the spaces that support them is vital to building trust. With trust comes solidarity, and the growing of shared meanings and values.

According to Landry and Wood, there are key public institutions where conditions can be created for interactions without forcing actions. They claim these spaces have 'strategic intent, careful planning, and skilled intervention to transform avoidance and indifference into engagement and co-operation'. In their view, places like museums, libraries, sports, the arts, and computer-mediated communication can be pre-disposed to being intercultural. This is because they are 'programmed' in light-touch ways to build on shared interests, common curiosities, active debate, disagreement, mediation and resolution. They serve to displace people from their cultural moorings, just enough for them to begin to see the world through the eyes of another, without forcing them onto the defensive.

In their study of Newham, a diverse borough of East London, Dines and Cattell illustrate that certain public spaces support culturally-based networks and promote a sense of pride. A key factor is how these spaces are perceived and valued. Unstructured cultural interactions provide experience and increase tolerance because they are unthreatening. They are spaces that harness the potential for maintaining and improving inter-cultural relations as sites where people, under the right circumstances or with the necessary encouragement, might come together. As everyday settings they offer a wide range of interests and attachments to place.

In their interview-based study of Newham, Dines and Cattell highlight the importance of key spaces that were valued by different cultures, including:

- Queens Market - a bustling, jostling market, which facilitated casual exchange and encouraged encounters between different cultural groups who would otherwise not come into contact with each other. It was generally recognised as a setting for developing tolerance.
- Green Street was known as the 'Asian' street; a busy shopping street that played a positive role in promoting place identity, a sense of pride, and supporting cultural networks, but not necessarily for promoting new intercultural encounters.
- A small neighbourhood park adjacent to a primary school, where meetings between parents in the welcoming lobby of the school led to greater shared use of the neighbouring park . Together, the school and the park had helped to bring different communities together
- Younger, single, Asian informants enjoyed visiting the West End and other places such as the shisha bars on Edgware Road, partly as a form of escape from their 'community' but mainly because such places offered opportunities for social

encounters and experiences that the local area did not provide.

- Neighbourhood and semi-domestic spaces, such as residential streets and shared forecourts for houses and flats provided the first point of contact with neighbours of different cultures. Echoing a practice once common to the East End, when sitting by the front step was a popular form of sociability, a white British woman had got to know her Asian and African Caribbean neighbours by sitting with her friend out on her front drive. A black British man who lived in a small block of flats had first encountered his white neighbours on the green space in front of the block. A Pakistani woman, who thought it simpler and safer to stay with one's cultural or religious group, nevertheless suggested that her habitual use of neighbourhood spaces over time was an instrumental factor in good relations with her largely white neighbours.
- The exchange of food was an important means for establishing and maintaining ties between different residents. People also indicated the key role that children played in drawing families together, which led to continued contact in local spaces.
- Informal games and sports in the neighbourhood park were seen by some residents as the principal means of encounter between young people.
- The new community centre provided reasons for contact and exchange across potential cultural divides
- Spaces of association, such as clubs or groups based around communities of interest provided key sites of engagement such as a day centre where the Albanian and Bosnian women could speak to compatriots but also where they were able to meet and work alongside people of different origins, such as Lithuanians, Pakistanis and Somalis
- A Sikh temple off Green Street was used by the market campaign group for its public meetings. This was seen as an

open, welcoming space. However, the relationships consolidated between people during these meetings were often initiated in the market itself and later fostered through their collective mobilisation over public space.

What this study shows is that those public spaces perceived to be of value gave diverse people the choice to undertake different degrees of 'togetherness' in the context of everyday, ordinary, routine activities. They were motivated by different needs. Most of all, the study emphasises that interaction can never be forced or false. It takes time to achieve familiarity as it is about people's habits in their public behaviour. It is the potential of these everyday spaces that needs to be harnessed. Their daily movements and interactions should be enjoyable and stimulating. Therefore, any spatial interventions should be about improving the conditions and circumstances for these intercultural interactions to take place. For example; improving the physical conditions at the school gate or bus stop to widen pavements, or adjusting a market's management regime. These are both interventions that take small steps, and start with people's existing behaviour and preferences.

Feeling safe and secure in a space is a vital precursor to fostering trust and encouraging new uses. Signs of crime and vandalism communicate disrespect and lack of care for residents. Until these are tackled, interventions aimed at more sophisticated integration goals will have only limited success.

There is also a policy dimension. Policies can encourage greater intercultural encounters in public space to support feeling safe and secure. One of the most innovative policy developments in recent years has been the Intercultural Cities Index. It is a tool developed by The Intercultural Cities Programme on behalf of the Council of Europe. They promote the adoption of city-wide Intercultural Policy, including intercultural public space policies. Phil Wood, consultant to the Intercultural Cities Programme, has written about the degree to which intercultural public space policies have been implemented in European cities. He shows correlations between residents' feeling of safety in the city and the adoption of intercultural space policies. What he reports is those cities are safer cities compared to those that do not have policies. There are exceptions to this rule, however. Wood argues that the empirical evidence from the Intercultural Cities Index suggests that policies that support the maintenance of open, safe, attractive and intercultural public spaces have localised benefits and positive effects on city performance.

Policies can also support the emergence of new communities or their continuous adaptation. Through spatial or activity-based interventions, local communities can be connected. They can open up and friendships can be established. In some neighbourhoods this has included the establishment of a joint vegetable gardening club, collective recycling, participation in neighbourhood radio or television channels. Exchanges occur between institutions or groups such as schools and theatres as well. These types of activities can lead to the sharing of concern and the creation of new networks of social capital. The focus is on citizen-led community-building approaches. Social innovation in public spaces galvanises the public to get involved. Civic action around issues of common interest, provides the emotional and intellectual outlets needed to help people form better relationships. Several commentators stress the importance of civic action. Landry and Wood, in particular, write extensively on the Intercultural Practitioner for which they list a new skills set:

- Cultural competence – the ability to reflect upon one's own culture and the culture of others

- Emotional and spiritual competence – the ability to be self-reflective, handle one's own emotions, empathise with others
- Linguistic and communicative competencies – the ability to listen to people, their stories, and to translate their aspirations into expert systems
- Civic competence – the ability to understand and act upon rights and responsibilities and be socially and morally responsible
- Creative competence – the ability to find different creative mediums for communities to express themselves

Policy-makers and practitioners working in diverse areas, and particularly when designing and managing public space, need to balance the seemingly contradictory cultural priorities of different communities. How are their different cultural values reflected in public spaces? In a report commissioned by the Commission for Racial Equality, Lownsbrough and Beunderman conclude four key recommendations:

- be flexible in the use of space, understand the grain of people's everyday lives and reflect it in the design of public space
- aim to create the setting for 'trusted' spaces, where people feel secure to take part in unfamiliar interactions
- foster positive interactions but don't promote them: take an indirect approach to changing behaviour
- embrace creativity and innovation in finding new and imaginative uses for spaces that will transform interactions between people

The focus is clearly not on the design challenges of public spaces alone. As we know, cosmetic interventions in public space such as new paving, elegant street furniture and improved lighting alone do not encourage underperforming public spaces.

Businesses fail, traffic dominates and anti-social behavior takes place in these spaces. What an intercultural approach to public space requires is that people are given the voice and opportunity to develop a shared future. Each individual feels they have something to contribute in shaping, making, using, and co-creating a shared space. The next section considers the benefits of co-creating public space.

Co-Design of Public Space

Co-design is, at its simplest, about decision-makers and stakeholders working together for the creation and implementation of a policy, service, or project. It meets the needs and wants of its beneficiaries. Collaborative (social) design is not intended as a substitute for government intervention, but as an opportunity for governments to understand their citizens' real life experiences as sites of learning and innovation. Co-design is an effort to reinvigorate public services. Burdened by increasing social complexity and a perpetuating lack of resources, co-design offers an alternative solution.

Traditional models of governing are becoming less powerful. Institutions are now exploring new governance practices. The shift of emphasis from service delivery and quantifiable outputs, to determining goals and directions jointly with users is proving more effective. Partnerships are created with beneficiaries themselves.

Co-design is based on central tenets such as participation, collaboration, and transparency. They reflect the local needs and values at the heart of a city's character. This way, public experiences can be transformed into powerful tools for addressing needs, stimulating critical thinking, and forming self-perpetuating networks of civic solidarity.

The process adds a political dimension of user empowerment and democratization to service delivery. It allows the creation of a framework for debate that releases the power of creativity to avoid the twin dangers of a lowest-common-denominator blandness, or extreme fragmentation. Because co-designed spaces are partly self-organised they tend to be much more flexible, responsive and therefore more able to simultaneously meet a diversity of needs. Public space works best when people are able to positively contribute to their everyday environments through their personal choice and actions.

The most innovative and successful examples of co-design have emerged from contexts where problems often appear to be intractable. Contexts where specialised thinking alone has proven not to be enough to address issues holistically and durably. Whereas engagement often ends at the consultation level, co-design implies long-term involvement in the design and delivery of the service itself. It allows participants to have a say in the way questions and projects are shaped. As a result, the end product typically better reflects customer needs, generates useful information, and creates a feeling of involvement and ownership. Co-design helps to counter the decline in trust in other people's behaviour. It generates a sense of community efficacy. Where principles of co-production are adopted, there tends to be a much higher confidence in other people's behaviour. A greater openness to a diversity of activities and people exists; people feel safe, but are more willing to take risks.

When the community is directly involved in entrepreneurial ventures, collaboration often takes on the characteristics of self-development projects. Collaborations spark opportunities for local organizations to make substantial investments in resources. This leads to enhanced economic and social vibrancy at the neighborhood level. Therefore, by regenerating the social fabric at the (hyper-) local level, actors in social economy; creative citizens in particular, effectively facilitate and invest in new approaches to social development. Leveraging their extensive networks of distributed enterprise, actors in the social economy blur the boundaries between production and consumption. They place an emphasis on long-term durability and care rather than unnecessary consumption.

To achieve success, co-design requires an enabling environment to focus on the equitable distribution of tools and spaces for self-knowledge and self-production. For Tims and Wright, authors of *So What Do You Do? Policy in the Age of Creativity* they claim policies and service should 'stimulate our individual capacities to create new possibilities, make new connections and tell a collective story.' Resources vary from creating learning opportunities and developing creativity as a basic human capacity to providing opportunities for micro-financing and project incubation.

Innovation hubs and public spaces are also key in encouraging knowledge exchanges. They help provide mentorship and support networks, stimulate spontaneous discovery, and disseminate collective stories. In short, Tims and Wright argue in favour of sparking conversations among actors. Conversations stimulate new kinds of leadership. They create a system of 'mass-story storage' to document civil society's journey into empowered participatory governance.

Collective will is the first step in ensuring that political authorities and their constituents mobilise resources that are relevant to the community's vision and help create a supportive culture. Service providers are given a strong incentive to share their power with beneficiaries. Similarly, mutual trust is crucial in ensuring a fair distribution of inputs and outcomes. Unequal power relations between stakeholders have to be addressed. Vulnerable demographics have to be given a chance to meaningfully participate. It is also of critical importance to design an enabling framework that empowers individuals to take control over their lives. This can happen through open and accessible debate. All views are of equal importance and priority.

In the discussion around public space design, increasingly the involvement of local people in the designing of a shared space ensures diverse needs are taken into account. In the case of the co-design process, the end user, or local resident, is given the position of expert of his/her experience. There is a shift of attitude from designing for users to designing *with* users. Local people participate in knowledge development, idea generation and concept development as experts of their place. Their knowledge of what works and what doesn't work for them in the way they live their everyday lives, how the public spaces accommodate their needs, and the functionality of the place at different times of the day, week, and the year, inform the design interventions. The social innovations in public space are rooted in the co-design process. Public space is the arena for debate, mediation, negotiation, and leadership in creating shared spaces. The next chapter will discuss the tools and techniques to break through social exclusion and provide the platform for co-design.

CHECKLIST

- Have you evaluated the public spaces in the neighbourhood for physical access, social access, visual access and access to activities?

- Have you evaluated the number, quality and sociability of third places, or hangouts at the heart of the community?

- Have you evaluated the variety and usability of public open spaces that meet the range of everyday needs: spaces to linger and transit; spaces that bring people together as well as retreat; green and hard landscapes?

- Have you evaluated the public spaces in relation to neighbourliness? Do they function as places that encourage social interaction, create memories and meaning, and are welcoming and safe?

- Have you evaluated whether the public spaces are inclusive and can accommodate multiple identities without singling one out, and accessible to all social groups?

- Have you evaluated the degree of sociability in public spaces that allow for people to stop to sit and chat, tamed traffic, developed new activities for teens and new kinds of park activities, improved safety and security, brought new kinds of people to the local neighbourhood centre, promoted new opportunities for social interaction and community pride by introducing activities from different cultures, provided safe routes to walk and bike around, established more effective community-based planning, fostered new types of businesses, and provided clean public restrooms?

- Have you evaluated the conditions in public spaces that provide weak ties between neighbours and serendipitous encounters?

- Have you evaluated and accounted for the range of potential spaces for social interaction including exchange spaces, productive spaces, spaces of service provision, activity spaces, democratic/participative spaces, staged spaces, in-between spaces and virtual spaces?

- Have you evaluated the experience of prejudice, racism and territoriality in your public spaces?

- Have you evaluated the location of community facilities in relation to the centre or edge of communities for better integration?

- Have you evaluated the range of key public institutions where conditions can be created for intercultural interactions and understanding without forcing actions such as museums, libraries, sports, the arts and computer-mediated communication?

- Have you evaluated the public spaces that support culturally-based networks or promote a sense of pride and identity based on the perceptions and values of a cultural cross-section of the place?

- Have you created an intercultural public space policy that supports the maintenance of open, safe, attractive and intercultural public spaces?

- Have you audited the competences and skills set required for intercultural practitioners in your neighbourhood?

- Have you evaluated whether there are enabling frameworks in place for the co-design of public space so that all cultures can have a say in the way public spaces are shaped, used and shared?

Chapter 3
What Makes People Get Along?

"Under the seeming disorder of the old city, wherever the old city is working successfully, is a marvelous order for maintaining the safety of the streets and the freedom of the city. It is a complex order. Its essence is intricacy of sidewalk use, bringing with it a constant succession of eyes. This order is all composed of movement and change, and although it is life, not art, we may fancifully call it the art form of the city and liken it to the dance — not to a simple-minded precision dance with everyone kicking up at the same time, twirling in unison and bowing off en masse, but to an intricate ballet in which the individual dancers and ensembles all have distinctive parts which miraculously reinforce each other and compose an orderly whole. The ballet of the good city sidewalk never repeats itself from place to place, and in any once place is always replete with new improvisations."

Jane Jacobs

In Chapter One, the importance of 'social capital' and the way it is played out in daily life through good will, reciprocity, fellowship, sympathy and social networks leads to the satisfaction of social needs and the improvement of living conditions. As Putnam points out ' social capital can have 'externalities' that affect the wider community, so that not all the costs and benefits of social connections accrue to the person making the contact....a well-connected individual in a poorly connected society is not as productive as a well-connected individual in a well-connected society. And even a poorly connected individual may derive some of the spill-over benefits from living in a well-connected society'. This chapter considers those benefits in more detail and ways in which social capital can be built up in a place so that it can be better socially connected.

The case for social mixing is set out in Landry and Wood's *The Intercultural City*. They mention a number of benefits for social mixing:

- Social mixing would nurture a spirit of emulation, motivate those less affluent, and provide greater opportunity for people to exercise choice to climb the social and economic ladder
- Living in close proximity with those of different social and economic backgrounds stimulates a more competitive aesthetic standard
- Socially mixed residential neigbourhoods promote intellectual and cultural cross-fertilisation leading to greater tolerance
- Mixing promotes social harmony by reducing social and racial tensions as a result of greater communication through interaction and raising levels of trust and greater understanding
- Mixing promotes social conflict considered important to individual psychological growth where disharmony can be reconciled
- Mixed residential areas improve the physical functioning of the city because different income groups support civic infrastructure
- A high degree of diverse facilities and housing types in a neighbourhood supports social stability

In today's world, neighbourhoods are increasingly zoned into enclaves that promote segregation rather than heterogeneity. In Chapter One, it was identified that fear and the perception of crime criminalises people from less advantaged and diverse backgrounds. At the same time, this fear has led to gated communities for the wealthy in which security and surveillance of privatised open spaces exclude the 'undesirables'. Only in cases where cultural difference is 'exoticised' has there been a thin level of tolerance, but no lasting understanding of difference. Underlying these trends are prejudices that seek to separate people. The next section focuses on understanding the mindsets that prevent people from interculturally mixing. Perceptions, attitudes and assumptions of prejudice need to be first addressed if bridging cultures is to achieved.

Why People Don't Get Along

For many global cities and global societies inequalities are rooted in prejudice. It is the fundamental way in which people make sense of the world around them. People mentally organise different groups of people into categories. It is a way to reinforce their group privilege over another. Invariably, prejudice results from a fear of strangers or feelings of superiority over others. It is formed by an attitude towards a particular social group based on incomplete or mistaken information. Generalisations, oversimplifications, and stereotyping about a group based on prior assumptions can lead to faulty beliefs. It leads to discrimination and inequality.

Some of the most well-known types of prejudice include racism, sexism, homophobia, nationalism, religious prejudice, and agism. A negative prejudice is when the attitude is hostile toward members of a group. A positive prejudice is when the attitude is unduly favorable toward a group. Groups that are the targets of prejudice may be distinguished by any one of several characteristics. Religion, ethnicity, language, social class, gender, physical abilities, age, or sexual orientation are forms of prejudice. Frequently they are distinguished by specific inherited physical characteristics such as skin colour. The way in which people categorise information tends to minimise differences between people within groups. The information exaggerates the differences between groups. People also tend to view members of 'outside groups' as being more homogenous than members of their own group, a phenomenon referred to as the 'out-group homogeneity bias'. This perception that all members of an out-group are alike holds true of all groups, whether based on race, nationality, religion, age, or other naturally occurring group affiliation.

Prejudice is such a basic part of a person's complex thought process that any one of many causes may be a factor. A person's appearance or unfamiliar social customs of others may be factors. Prejudice exists not only at the personal individual level, but also at the collective societal level. All human societies have prejudice in some form and to some degree. In fact many societies have multiple prejudices both at the individual and group levels, therefore determining the cause of prejudice in any single person is difficult. Most people do not willingly reveal their prejudices or the reasons for them, if they are even aware of their prejudices at all. Some people may have become prejudiced through some traumatic event they experienced in their lives. Others are simply conforming to the society in which they live, expressing the same prejudices as parents, popular political leaders, employers, or the media.

As there are many causes of prejudice, there can be many forms of prejudicial expression, the most common of which is discrimination. Discrimination is the unfair treatment of people simply because they are different from the dominant group in society. Prejudice and discrimination cause inequality especially when minorities are readily identified.

Reversing Prejudice through contact

One of the basic rationales is that prejudice may be reduced as one learns more about different cultures. Placing people into contexts where they become more empathetic to members of other cultural groups is one method that has shown considerable success in reversing prejudice. By imagining themselves in the same situation, people are able to think about how they would react and gain a greater understanding of other people's actions.

A number of hypotheses exist that examine the nature of inter-cultural relations. The most widely accepted is Allport's 'contact hypothesis' based on the reconceptualization of cultural group categories. This approach reconceptualises 'in-groups' and 'out-groups' in a way that constructs collective categories to which people belong. It reduces prejudice and promotes positive attitudes towards the out-group under certain conditions. Allport claims that when people are given an opportunity to communicate with others, they are able to understand and appreciate different points of views involving their way of life. The key is to manage this communication and mediate any conflicts. Allport identifies 5 conditions for positive contact:

- Equal status: Both groups must engage equally in the relationship. Members of the group should have similar backgrounds, qualities, and characteristics. Differences in academic backgrounds, wealth, skill, or experiences should be minimised if these qualities will influence perceptions of prestige and rank in the group.
- Common goals: Both groups must work on a problem/task and share this as a common goal, sometimes called a 'superordinate goal', a goal that can only be attained if the

members of two or more groups work together by pooling their efforts and resources.

- Intergroup cooperation: Both groups must work together for their common goals without competition. Groups need to work together in the pursuit of common goals.
- Support of authorities, law or customs: Both groups must acknowledge some authority that supports the contact and interactions between the groups. The contact should encourage friendly, helpful, egalitarian attitudes and condemn in group-out group comparisons.
- Personal interaction: The contact situation needs to involve informal, personal interaction without group members. Members of the conflicting groups need to mingle with one another. Without this criterion they learn very little about each other and cross-group friendships do not occur.

The interaction cycle takes a more psychological needs approach to understanding the conditions for positive contact based on a person's familiar internal world, their identity and values, as well as the unfamiliar interactions that lead to wider benefits:

- Grounding: interactions with close and familiar people that help confirm and consolidate a person's identity and values
- Strokes: interactions with familiar but less close people that consolidate a person's confidence as a member of a wider group
- Opportunity: interactions that open up to new people and that might lead to benefit for the person and for the other person
- Growth: interactions that open a person up to new people and that through discussion, debate and learning lead to the person achieving a new and enhanced understanding of the world to the extent that their identity and values are changed

Other theories for intercultural relations include the 'opportunity hypothesis'. It contends that the occurrence of cross-cultural friendships increases as the opportunities for them increase in contexts like multicultural schools. When the proportion of minorities increases, or where there are several groups present, the opportunity to form cross-cultural friendships increases significantly.

In contrast there are theories that identify why people would not interact. 'Similarity-attraction hypothesis' claims individuals are more likely to prefer to seek out people with whom they share salient characteristics. The 'culture-distance hypothesis' predicts the greater the cultural gap between people the more difficulties they will experience interacting. Another theory is based on 'civility towards difference' where people may be offended by differences in physical abilities, beauty, skin colour and hair texture, dress style, demeanour, income, sexual preferences, etc., but will act in a civil manner. This form of appreciation of diversity is based on treating people universally the same. It can emerge from indifference to diversity rather than from specific appreciation of it. Others caution against the positive effects of regular contact in improving intercultural understanding and shifting prejudiced perceptions. Indeed, some studies have shown that stereotypes and racism towards cultural diversity can co-exist with daily interactions in diverse neighbourhoods.

In his detailed study of the cause of the Bradford Riots, Ted Cantle was the first to claim how different cultures were living parallel lives. He identified five forms of interactions that measured the health of cross-cultural relationships:

- Intra-associational: integrated and multiple identity. Associations are open to people of different backgrounds and facilitate interchange and cooperation within the organisation, and promote social cohesion

- Inter-associational: networked single identity. Associations represent separate and distinct interests on an inclusive and single identity with associations formed by networks of separate bodies and which is less desirable for social cohesion
- Social incidental: arising from everyday activities. Interaction between individuals meeting through shopping, traveling or leisure activities, at an individual level, with organisation
- Social organisational: arising from planned and organised activity. Interaction by participating in sporting, music, drama and arts, which involves group activities, generally organised around clubs and societies and desirable for bridging capital
- Structural cross-cultural contact: This will depend upon the extent to which schools and housing are segregated, employment opportunities are linked to particular groups, and market factors create divisions which militate against cross cultural engagement. The greater the segregation, the weaker the social cohesion

Promoting Values for Bridging Cultures

Several commentators have suggested that it is the horizontal relationship between citizens, residents and local people with each other at the scale of the neighbourhood which creates a wider sense of common interest. People need to share things in common in order to live together. Several factors, in particular, are critical:

- Trust: people must trust one another to comply with the rules

- Solidarity: people must still recognise the value of contributing to the common good even when they don't directly benefit as a result
- Empowerment: People feel they have a voice which is listened to and are involved in processes that affect them. They have the power to take actions and initiate change themselves
- Participation: people take part in social and community activities
- Associational activity and Common purpose: people co-operate with each other through the formation of formal and informal groups to further their interests
- Supporting networks and reciprocity: People and organisations co-operate to support one another for either mutual or one-sided gain. An expectation that help would be given to or received from others when needed
- Collective norms and values: people share common norms and values. They tolerate and respect other people's norms and values.
- Safety: people feel safe in their neighbourhood and are not restricted in their use of public space by fear
- Belonging: people feel connected to their neighbours and place

We know that public spaces are vitally important for that, because they are where people often encounter one another. These values, such as trust and solidarity, are often built partly through familiarity. The gradual breaking down of the barriers of 'otherness', and the recognition of shared interests and a common humanity between strangers builds familiarity over time. For the same reason, the places where people interact with the state plays an essential part in building people's trust in the state. When it comes to diversity and change, particularly in communities which are experiencing tensions and rapid rates of mobility, trust becomes an essential element for building relationships.

Dispelling myths and stories about people in public space

So far in this chapter it is evident that to reverse prejudices that undermine social cohesion and bridging cultures, it is important to create the conditions for greater cross-cultural interaction. Public spaces are capable of providing either a positive or negative arena for social interaction. Examples of positive ideas for social interaction that bring people together across cultural divides are the focus of this book. To dispel the myths people have of 'others', it becomes critical for public space projects to consider ways for notional barriers and perceptions to be broken down.

Time is required to engage with local people to approach conflicts and prejudices. The need is to understand diversity and recognise all humans have some universal needs in common. In conflict mediation approaches it is important for cultural groups to self-identify their prejudices. This allows groups to choose to resolve the conflict. Community workshops should focus on individuals and social groups examining the nature of their assumptions and perceptions. It is followed by a meeting with all participants in the conflict to develop shared understanding.

There may be other more creative ways to explore differences within a positive rather than deficit model. Storytelling is a powerful tool, as are cross-cultural events. Here are a couple of examples:

- Stories that identify different people's roots and share their pride in their heritage with others.

- Inviting friends from different backgrounds to experience the joy of different traditions and customs.
- Planning family outings to diverse neighborhoods in and around the community and to visit local museums, galleries and exhibits that celebrate art forms of different cultures
- Visiting important landmarks in the area associated with the struggle for human and civil rights such as museums, public libraries and historical sites
- Identifying personal heroes and positive role models
- Reading and encouraging children to read books that promote understanding of different cultures as well as those that are written by authors of diverse backgrounds
- Researching family trees and record the immigration and settlement experience

CHECKLIST:

- Have you assessed how socially mixed your neighbourhood is in terms of different people living in close proximity, diverse facilities and housing types that support neighbourhood stability and provide greater opportunity for people to exercise choice to climb the social and economic ladder?

- Have you asked local people if they have prejudices against others in their neighbourhood as a result of fear of strangers or feelings of superiority over others?

- Have you got statistics that measure the level of discrimination and racist hostility in your neighbourhood?

- Have you assessed the nature of social contact on the basis of equal status, common goals, intergroup cooperation, the support of authorities, law or customs, and informal personal interactions?

- Have you assessed the reasons why people are in contact based on grounding, strokes, opportunity, and growth, and whether they are balanced?

- Have you assessed the types of engagement and social contact based on intra-associational contact, inter-associational contact, social incidental contact, social organisational contact, and structural cross-cultural contact, and whether it is balanced?

- Have you assessed the level of trust, solidarity, empowerment, participation, associational activity and common purpose, supporting networks and reciprocity, collective norms and values, safety and sense of belonging are present in your neighbourhood?

- Have you considered creative ways to dispel myths people have of each other in your neighbourhood?

PART TWO

Chapter 4
Neighbourhood Hangouts

"There is no logic that can be superimposed on the city; people make it, and it is to them, not buildings, that we must fit our plans."
Jane Jacobs

People attract people. This statement was first coined by William H. Whyte in his detailed study of *The Social Life of Small Urban Spaces*. Whyte attributes the 'people attraction' behaviour to a number of factors but most surprisingly he found people 'self-congest'. People like busy places. He observed how conversations tended to happen in places with the greatest pedestrian flows and the densest opportunities for encounter; on street corners, along main pedestrian paths, in the middle of a traffic stream, near objects like statues or fountains, along a curb. In short, people's movements are one of the greatest spectacles of a place. People like to watch other people. People are drawn to places where other people go. It is this type of behaviour, and its location on busy pathways, that is conducive to 'hanging out'.

What is a hang out?

What is it about places that attract people? This chapter is about neighbourhood 'hangouts' – places where people from different cultures meet. Hangouts are meeting places. Every vibrant and cohesive neighbourhood should have a few hangouts where everyone feels welcome and can strike up a conversation with their neighbour. Sociologist Ray Oldenburg calls neighbourhood hangouts a 'third place'; places that are for socialising and are relaxing and fulfilling. They are places that balance between domestic and work life. Oldenburg's central thesis is that increasingly contemporary domestic life consists of isolated nuclear families or single people living alone. The work environment is similarly solitary, anti-social and competitive. Oldenburg argues people need the release and stimulation that more sociable realms provide. His term 'third place' signifies 'the great variety of public places that host regular, voluntary, informal and happily anticipated gatherings of individuals beyond the realms of home and work'. Third places are often specific to cultures such as the pub in the UK, outdoor cafes in French and Italian towns, coffee houses in Austrian cities, and beer gardens in Germany. More recently, third places accommodate multiple complimentary uses that together increase footfall and attraction; for example the location of Starbucks coffee shops in bookstores.

For Oldenburg the core qualities of third places are:

- Being 'neutral ground', where individuals can come and go as they please
- Being highly inclusive, accessible and without formal criteria of membership
- Their 'taken-for-granted-ness' and low profile
- Being open during and outside office hours
- Being characterised by a 'playful mood'
- Providing psychological comfort and support
- With conversation their 'cardinal and sustaining' activity, providing 'political fora of great importance'

In every neighbourhood there are either existing places or places of potential which could be transformed into neighbourhood hangouts. These are public spaces that help bridge differences through associations and intercultural contact. The next section examines how a neighbourhood space can become a hangout.

What are the conditions for a successful hang out?

Many community-building processes are based on creating third places. Third places are most successfully created by 'triangulation': this simply refers to the way elements in a public place build on one another, creating something more than the sum of its parts. It is synergy. PPS calls this synergy the 'Power of Ten', meaning that if there are at least ten things you can do in a particular spot, it will likely become a popular destination for people in the neighborhood. As an example they describe this scenario: 'Take a humble spot in your neighborhood - a bus stop or a branch library - and consider how you could gradually fashion it into a hub of public activity. Add a bench to the bus stop, then a trash receptacle and a drinking fountain, and it changes the whole feel of the corner. A regular Saturday morning story time, along with a community message board out front and a playground for tots, transforms the library into a community center. Then see what happens at either location when a coffee shop with sidewalk tables opens, some public art is created, and vendors arrive selling ice cream or garden produce. Voilà! You've got a great hangout, a place you'll visit even when you're not taking the bus or looking for a book. You show up because you know something will be happening there'.

In her study of the 'superdiverse' London Borough of Hackney, Susanne Wessendorf, describes the parochial realm. She characterises the parochial realm by more communal relations among neighbours, with colleagues in the workplace, or acquaintances through associations or schools. What distinguishes the public realm, in her view, is that in the public realm people meet strangers, whereas in the parochial realm, like a corner shop or a market where traders and customers meet on a regular basis, social relations become habitual and frequent. The differentiation between the public, parochial and private realm is particularly useful when thinking about the degree to which interactions between people of different backgrounds are meaningful and contribute to intercultural understanding. She describes how the weekly coffee morning in the local primary school creates opportunities to socialise with people of diverse backgrounds. The mothers attending the coffee morning emphasised that having children facilitated social contacts with other parents. Conversations often focused on those shared interests like gardening, cooking and education, rather than their differences. Wessendorf concludes by saying: 'while not talking about difference could be interpreted as a way to avoid tensions, it could also be explained with the existence of a general acceptance of people who are different and a sense that as long as people interact and are friendly, things are fine.'

Another ethnographic study of 'Nick's Caff' on the Walworth Road in London by Suzanne Hall describes the importance of this meeting place to the local neighbourhood. Hall talks about the Caff as a place where 'foreigner' and 'local' sit literally and conceptually at the same table. Nick, the café owner, is a second generation migrant from Cyprus. His father opened the Caff in the 1960s, and it has become a regular and sustained institution on the Walworth Road throughout the demographic changes. Today it is a superdiverse neighbourhood. The study showed how socially organised the Caff is spatially and temporally. It allows people to claim a place to sit within the 'rhythm of the day'. Hall records the 'performances' that regulate conversations, eye contact, distance, and intimacy. She notes 'the caff was a place to go to regularly, either spontaneously or as part of a routine. It was a place where one could do nothing much without being moved on; there was no institutional setting or formal membership required for being there. One may go through the formality of ordering a cup of tea, but more importantly the Caff was a place where one could spend time and take your time.' What both studies of Hackney and the Walworth Road show is the importance of places accommodating opportunities to linger and that provide a shared interest.

The Power of Ten concept has transformed the perceptions of public spaces. One case study is a street in New Haven where a meeting place was created by a savvy developer, Joel Schiavone. Chapel Street in the downtown of New Haven, Connecticut, had by the 1980s suffered severe urban decline with only five percent of the area's residential and commercial spaces being occupied. Schiavone was inspired to invest in a number of small interventions without making the street look radically different. He convinced city officials to undo the damage of an earlier street-widening project by expanding the pavements so that Chapel Street felt like a place you'd want to hang out. As a result, a café expanded with outdoor seating, then two more cafés opened, and a newspaper vendor set up shop. Today, Chapel Street is thriving, a hub for people to use the place throughout the day and week. As a result of uses that began to attract footfall, other establishments began to have confidence in opening up leading to the opening of nightclubs, restaurants, several theatres, and shops selling everything from bicycles to jewelry. 'The whole thing is like a mosaic,' Schiavone explains. 'Each piece needs to be carefully considered: street furniture, flowerboxes, a particular tenant for a storefront, tree plantings. If it's done right, all these things come together to create a real neighborhood.'

Experimenting with Social Innovation: PieLab

The PieLab project is a particularly inspiring story of fourteen designers who worked together to address a common concern negatively affecting everyday life in Maine, US. They identified the degradation of healthy and supportive communities. Free pie, a hearty and traditional local dish, was their response to this concern.

Their first intervention was to set up a pop-up pie stand on a central corner in downtown. They served over 200 slices of pie to hungry locals. Each slice was served on a real ceramic place and eaten with a real fork, encouraging people to hang around and interact with neighbours while enjoying the pie.

This very successful first event encouraged the designers to initiate the Free Pie Movement. It was a way of motivating others to offer the same simple gestures within their communities. The idea took off, and similar events began to happen in neighbourhoods across the US including Atlanta, Brooklyn, Richmond, Columbus, and Washington DC. The idea became synonymous with a multifaceted approach to small business. It addressed the need for united and empowered community in a way that is self-perpetual and fun. They called it PieLab.

A small number of the designers who had set up PieLab relocated to Greensboro, Alabama, a place that had suffered from economic decline. Within three weeks of arriving the team had converted an old home into a real, live, and functioning pie shop. The shop was fitted out with recycled furniture, kitchenware, and signs.

When they opened the shop up to visitors, the people started to come. They were from all backgrounds and ages. At very low cost they could enjoy a slice of pie and a drink, and some good conversation. All revenue generated from the pie sales went back into subsidising more pies. The concept was simple: pie brings people together, conversations happen, ideas are created, and the result is positive change through design. At the same time, PieLab provided the perfect space for local people and the designers to interact, share stories and get acquainted. Projects and ideas were then generated based on a real understanding of the community's assets and needs.

Image of PieLab as a third place for community conversations

Within a few short months, a local not-for-profit housing resource centre invested in PieLab transforming it from a pop-up to a High Street business and a commercial kitchen. This new growth brought with it further opportunities for community initiatives, like retail and hospitality training for local youth, a small business workshop programme, a place to host community events like open mic, ballroom dancing, artist gallery shows, etc. The design studio also worked to develop additional projects for community engagement such as BikeLab, a bike-and-build initiative to promote cycling by youth, and other such projects.

Image of PieLab as a shop front on the high street to hang out

PieLab Social Innovation Checklist

This section aims to determine where the social innovation in this project lies. The aim is to provide a benchmark for your hangouts in your neighbourhoods.

- *Does PieLab provide a product, service or model that addresses pressing unmet needs to improve people's lives and provide the solutions to social cohesion?* Yes. PieLab provided a product and a service aimed at addressing the concern of the degradation of healthy and supportive communities in their locality.

- *Does PieLab start from the presumption that people are competent interpreters of their own lives and competent solvers of their own problems?* Yes. A bunch of fourteen local designers took their own initiative to make the change based on their participation in Project M, John Bielenberg's design-for-good movement – a source of inspiration and motivation for them.

- *Does PieLab lead to new or improved capabilities and relationships and better use of assets and resources?* Yes. The team of designers were able to set up a pop-up pie stand, pop-up shop, set up socially-minded enterprises, run a commercial business using local physical, economic and social assets and resources.

- *Was Pie Lab driven by a sharp external push that galvanised the will to change?* Yes. Pielab's concept is based on the idea that pie brings people together, conversations happen, ideas are created, and the result is positive change.

- *Did there emerge a strong internal capacity to develop innovations and put them into practice through the right leadership, structures and organisational culture?* Yes. The team of designers organised themselves in such a way that allowed the transferability of their ideas through the Free Pie Movement and later into pop-ups and commercial business. The organisational structure was transferable.

- *Did the leaders mobilise the right external resources by galvanising stakeholder support, partnerships and funding and mobilising a set of networks to embed change?* Yes. They were initially supported by Project M and later by the Hale Empowerment and Revitalisation Organisation to fund the growth and application of their ideas.

- *What was the nature of citizenship engagement in relation to understanding needs and problems, understanding larger patterns and trends, co-developing solutions and crowdsourcing solutions?* The nature of citizen engagement was based on local understanding of the problem and wider trends, and co-developing solutions through PieLab as a space for sharing ideas that matter to the community.

- *To what extent has the project completed the social innovation cycle: addressed critical issue; developed several approaches; mobilised teams to pilot approach; mainstreamed to scale up; disseminated to other fields and sectors?* PieLab has scaled up its service from pop-up to commercial business but has yet to transfer its business model and ideas beyond Alabama, and into other sectors.

Chapter 5
Programming Public Spaces

"You can't rely on bringing people downtown,
you have to put them there."
Jane Jacobs

Public spaces are better understood from the perspective of people. A new town square could be carefully and beautifully designed, but there is no guarantee that people would come and use it. People have different motivations and needs of public space. What becomes critical is the experience created by people's interaction with other people, and the uses in the public space. What this shift in understanding the value of public space entails is that public space has to be assessed in terms of how well it supports 'public experiences'. Belonging, friendship, community, adventure, reflection, learning, and economic exchange are some of those experiences. The sociability of public spaces lies in their provision of activities, experiences, and comfort that attract people to it. For Mean and Tims, public space is any space where there are shared uses for a diverse range of activities by a range of different people, regardless of appearance or whether it is in public ownership. It is what goes on within a space that is important.

Interaction and conviviality in neighbourhoods of high cultural diversity does not always happen naturally. Studies have found that balancing and responding to people's needs sometimes requires a good deal of choreography and guardianship of a space. Choreographers may be paid park wardens, volunteers such as Friends of the Park, Town Teams, or youth workers. Their role is to reinvigorate these public open spaces in ways that build a collective sense of place. Places must be welcoming to a diverse range of users, and choreographers help keep the peace. Choreographers can sometimes be pivotal in encouraging bridging capital. One case is Pearson Park in Hull where turf conflict between the local white youth and incoming Kurdish refugees became a big concern. The council appointed two park rangers. One ranger was a Kurd. He was able to negotiate peace between the gangs. The pavilion in the park that had been jealously guarded by elderly men was opened up to the wider community. Today the pavilion is used for a variety of intercultural leisure activities, Kurdish and English language lessons, a job club and Hate Crime Report Centre. Large gatherings and barbecues for different cultures meet there. The best places encourage self-policing and a degree of self-organisation. They are places where people create activities, where they can organise the space for themselves, and have ownership over it.

Types of Social Happenings

Programming social events, celebrations, gatherings, shows and cultural festivals are ways to bring people together to focus on fun and entertainment. Combining physical attraction with the excitement of activity is the recipe for success. This helps people connect in an informal, often random way. A sense of community and shared interest grows in functioning public spaces.

The types of activities that attract people because of their entertainment value mostly involve sport, play, art, culture, and food. These types of activities can be enjoyed regardless of age, gender, or cultural background. They provide opportunities for cross-cultural learning and have the capacity to build communities through 'doing' and 'sharing in the experience'.

Sport, for example, has been shown to build understanding within and across cultures. This is only possible within the context of interdependence i.e. teams were a mix of different cultures and have had to rely on each other to win. Non-competitive contexts offer greater racial tolerance. In Leicester UK, The Voluntary Action Leicester: Asylum Seekers and Refugees Sports Development Project, promotes sport as its primary method of drawing them into social networks. The focus on football and netball has addressed gender equity. What they found is sport leadership training has been useful in enhancing other competences such as language and communication skills, improving self-esteem, and enhancing employability. Ashram Moseley Housing Association have successfully used sport to build community spirit and self-esteem in young people within its diverse tenants base.

The curiosity and questioning about the way the world is most commonly associated with artists. They serve as an intercultural platform. Art provides a space for different cultures to share a similar experience of discovery in which they can detach momentarily from their own identities. Successful examples of artists projects have worked well in exploring difficult questions. One example is the Burnley Youth Theatre exploring the deep-rooted nature of white racism during the 2001 riots. The young people from both the white and Asian communities made a play about their vision for the future. They presented three possibilities for Burnley in a hundred years. This is an example of imaginative theatre enabling young men to confront their deepest fears and create a future through their art form.

With many artists emerging from different cultural backgrounds, minority arts has been considered a separate genre. In an attempt to mainstream minority arts, the construction of Rich Mix, a £20 million project in East London, is the first intercultural innovation for the arts. The building sets out to redefine a cultural institution as a place of intercultural experiences and the interchange of ideas, people and cultures.

Festivals and carnivals are the most visible intercultural events. Carnivals like the Caribbean-led Nottinghill Carnival and the Asian-inspired Mela, or the Sikh Vaisakhi Festivals attract large crowds that are increasingly diverse. However, there are critics that claim many of these carnivals have lost their authenticity and are in fact promoted as 'exotic experiences' rather than as an opportunity for intercultural participation. Where festivals and carnivals are opportunities to create British hybrids of music, song, dance, film, and theatre, there is more scope for creativity and inclusivity. The Fusion Project in Berlin, Neukoelln, which is a densely populated district in central Berlin, converts one residential street into an intercultural social space. FUSIONSTREET has ever since randomly offered parties, concerts, dance performances, flea markets, art and theatre involving children attending the adjacent schools but also their family, friends, neighbours or just passers-by. More than a third of its residents originate from countries other than Germany. FUSION emphasises the arts (e.g. music, theatre, dance, costume design, making masks, sculpture, film and photography) as a means by which, many people, especially young locals, can represent their own realities to others. The festival has grown into a space where different cultures meet and merge into something new.

Food is always a popular draw for people from different cultures. Not only does food represent deeply-held traditions and customs as part of self-identity, it is also an opportunity for creativity. Sharing food builds trust and reciprocity. One example is the Big Lunch. It is a UK-wide initiative when on a summer's day people sit down together for lunch in the middle of streets, around tower blocks, and on any patch of common ground. Since starting the Big Lunch in 2009, around a million people have turned out each year for the biggest collection of street parties. It is used as an excuse to get people making contact, sharing stories, skills and interests. Instigated by the Eden Project, the vision was the day after the Big Lunch people would be able to walk down their street and know their neighbours.

Programming events can also take place at the level of the urban block. In the US, in Davis California, people came together to create a Common House where everyone in the block can gather for meals, activities, or just watch the big game on TV. The project is part of a vision for co-housing, popular in northern European countries and relatively new in the US. Residents combine private and community living as part of a communal spirit. Other shared facilities include gardens, fields, workshops, children playrooms, libraries, and volleyball courts.

Play is another powerful attractor of people. For a child, play is vital to their well-being and development in their formative years. Play helps develop a sense of risk, improves confidence and self-esteem and teaches how to socialise. At the scale of the neighbourhood, play brings people together. It breaks down social barriers and contributes to a healthier society. As in Susanne Wessendorf's example, parents get better related through school-based association and in the school playground. Play teaches children how to negotiate what they want, imitate their peers, and take on leadership roles. Studies have shown that with less adult intervention and direct supervision, children can build robust relationships across cultural boundaries. They can influence their parents in building bridges. Playgrounds are important opportunities for intercultural interactions, as are activities focused on playing.

For teenagers, exercise and fitness can be a big motivator. In an inspiring example, a former gang member and prisoner, London-born Terroll 'Boost' Lewis turned his life around through exercise and fitness. He started doing street workouts in a local park near his estate where he lived. At first, he would work out in the children's playground because he didn't have money to sign up to a gym. Then he started inviting people who couldn't afford a gym membership to come and train with him. The group grew stronger and he started to promote street fitness & outdoor training on all his social networking sites. He founded Block Workout, a street workout movement that seeks to cultivate a healthy lifestyle by making use of everyday items and surroundings. He started to hold community training sessions in Kennington Park, South London. Terroll's work is centred around helping young people improve themselves and keep out of trouble. He encourages deadlifts over drugs, bench-presses over brawls, and by equipping them with an early determination to get and stay fit. The achievements of Terroll's fitness in the park has had a significant positive impact on relationships between post-code youth gangs in the area. Not only young men, but also girls have joined his sessions in the park. The crime rate has decreased, and young people can see the benefits of focusing their attention on staying positive and doing something for themselves. Today, Terroll has founded the Brixton Street Gym, Block Workout's first home.

Experimenting with Social Innovation: Burnside Park 'Lighter Quicker Cheaper', Providence

The Burnside Park project is a particularly inspiring story of how a downtown Providence Park was transformed from a place people didn't want to stay in, into a crowded and bustling place for people of all backgrounds and ages. At the time, the space was dominated by a small number of unemployed adults. There was little reason for other residents or visitors to want to spend time there. The park was well maintained. Locals mostly walked through it on their way somewhere else. There wasn't much incentive to stay. Local civic leaders identified an opportunity to revitalise the downtown public spaces that included Burnside Park. Their vision was to integrate these key public spaces with the RIPTA bus transit hub close by. Their immediate response was to set up a series of public workshops. The workshops began developing a long-term vision to connect all the key downtown public spaces together and to fill them with a diverse range of uses and activities.

The first intervention was to take an approach PPS had first pioneered called 'Lighter, Quicker, Cheaper' (LQC). This approach is experimental. Short-term improvements to a place are tested and refined with the aim of making positive changes. The changes can be accomplished in a short time. It offers exceptional flexibility and serves as an ever-evolving means to build lasting change. LQC is lower risk and lower cost. It capitalises on the creative energy of the community to efficiently generate new uses and revenue for places in transition. LQC projects allow people to try out new things. If one thing doesn't work, they try something else. If the project is a success, people build on it. The first LQC strategy in Burnside Park was to launch an ambitious and diverse programming schedule. The programme included a relocated farmer's market, a new craft market, regular performances, and special events. The coalition leading the project comprised of the council, RIPTA, and Cornish Associates, and they employed a full-time programme manager.

This very successful first event encouraged the coalition to launch a suite of family programmes. Partnering with local parenting blog KIDOinfo, they organised a weekly outdoor *Storytime* programme for families in Burnside Park. The following year they added *Art in the Park* and a mobile playground. Although many of the activities were geared to children, the organisers were intent on creating activities that would appeal to a wide range of users. By focusing on the children they were able to attract the parents. They found that even adults who didn't have children were getting engaged.

Image of Burnside Park celebrations for adults

The idea of starting with simple low-cost interventions such as the mobile playground, hula-hoops, balls, and an inflatable bowling kit to encourage people to start playing began to create a sense of community. The appeal of the park radiated across the city, with families coming from the east side and the west side of town.

Image of Burnside Park being used by families

The concept of LQC pioneered by PPS was simple: engaging multiple uses for a space, trying things out, seeing who the space attracts, and who will invest in the space in various ways. LQC has become a preferred approach when budgets are constrained and has been used across the US and beyond.

Burnside Park and its surrounding public spaces received further funding to support the development of both the short and long-term visions. As the plan developed, they continued to engage with the local community through a series of presentations and workshops. Plans focused on a wide range of issues from programming and management plans to an extensive redesign of the existing multi-modal transit hub with RIPTA. These efforts culminated in a massive public event, the FirstWorks Festival, which showcased local and international performers.

Despite all of this success, there were still many challenges for a group with a small staff and an even smaller budget. They successfully won funding to develop a set of improvements and amenities that would take the park to the next level. The team decided the best strategy is to develop a small building with a deck as a home base. It would have a deck that could support activities in different ways. It would provide shelter and work spaces for other activities, and it could be used to store any play equipment and materials. The building would be the focus for community-based activities like an open air reading room, display artwork, and become a landmark for activity in the park. The spaces around it could be used for new movable seating and to define play areas. Eventually the place could support a small food vendor as well. Since opening, the Imagination Center has had a catalytic impact on Burnside Park as a place where families now visit every single day the programme is running. The Imagination Center has become a home inside the park.

Image of Burnside Park being used by children

What this programme of uses and activities has provided is a space the community can call their own. The on-going public workshops have shifted local people from being 'audience members' to co-creators. The programmes bring people to the park. The park has now become even more. It has become a landmark for meeting with people using the park for impromptu meetings, as the starting point for group bike rides, and as a venue for artistic and political expression. The park has become an integrated part of people's everyday lives and has deepened the sense of community.

Burnside Park LQC Social Innovation Checklist

This section aims to determine where the social innovation in this project lies. The aim is to provide a benchmark for how to activate your public spaces in your neighbourhoods.

- *Does Burnside Park LQC provide a product, service or model that addresses pressing unmet needs to improve people's lives and provide the solutions to social cohesion?* Yes. The Lighter Quicker Cheaper approach to Burnside Park provides a model aimed at addressing the concern of an underused park that had negative perceptions in local people's minds. People did not want to stay in the park.

- *Does Burnside Park LQC start from the presumption that people are competent interpreters of their own lives and competent solvers of their own problems?* Yes. The public were involved right from the very start in developing the short and long term visions for the park.

- *Does Burnside Park LQC lead to new or improved capabilities and relationships and better use of assets and resources?* Yes. Using small budgets, the LQC model in Burnside is resourceful. A combination of great ideas to revitalise the park, clear leadership, a small team to deliver the programme, and on-going engagement with the public served to improve capabilities and relationships.

- *Was Burnside Park LQC driven by a sharp external push that galvanised the will to change?* Yes. Burnside Park, along with the surrounding key downtown public spaces were underused and unsafe. This was the motivation by civic leaders to do something about it.

- *Did there emerge a strong internal capacity to develop innovations and put them into practice through the right leadership, structures and organisational culture?* Yes. The coalition working with a team of designers and a programme manager organised themselves to make things happen, in spite of budgetary challenges.

- *Did the coalitions mobilise the right external resources by galvanising stakeholder support, partnerships and funding and mobilising a set of networks to embed change?* Yes. They sought funding on a number of occasions to develop the programme in the park and to build a home base for them.

- *What was the nature of citizenship engagement in relation to understanding needs and problems, understanding larger patterns and trends, co-developing solutions and crowdsourcing solutions?* The nature of citizen engagement was based on local understanding of the problem and wider trends, and co-developing solutions through the planning and design process.

- *To what extent has the project completed the social innovation cycle: addressed critical issue; developed several approaches; mobilised teams to pilot approach; mainstreamed to scale up; disseminated to other fields and sectors?* LQC has scaled up its model to other similar spaces in other cities internationally. It may not have been disseminated to other fields and sectors due to appropriateness.

Chapter 6
Socialising Public Spaces

"The more successfully a city mingles everyday diversity of uses and users in its everyday streets, the more successfully, casually (and economically) its people thereby enliven and support well-located parks that can thus give back grace and delight to their neighborhoods instead of vacuity. "
Jane Jacobs

Public spaces can provide the 'circumstances' for social interaction by their design and layout. The arrangement, connectivity, and props within a physical space can encourage casual or serendipitous encounters. Jane Jacobs, in her writing of the failure of modern town planning in *The Death and Life of Great American Cities,* wrote about the fundamental connection between place and diversity. She said diversity corresponds to physical forms and patterns that maintain human interactions. For here diversity was a mix of uses, including variety in 'cultural opportunities', the inclusion of a 'variety of scenes', and a 'great variety [in] population and other users.

Jacobs drew conclusive remarks of the effect on design of public space on human diversity. She claimed public space is the basis of well-functioning, vital and healthy cities. Her design propositions included places with a mix of primary uses, mixed ages of building stock, short urban blocks, and the concentration of people and activity. What counted for Jane Jacobs was the 'everyday, ordinary performances in mixing people', forming complex 'pools of use' that would be capable of producing something greater than the sum of their parts. Diversity increases interactions among multiple urban components. A 'close grained' diversity of uses provides 'constant mutual support'. Planning must, Jacobs argued, ' become the science and art of catalyzing and nourishing these close-grained working relationships.' This proximity of uses and people allowed for natural surveillance – the capacity for people to keep an eye on things as part of their everyday routines. To promote natural surveillance, buildings should front public space. People should be able to look out of their windows directly on to the public realm in front of them.

Natural surveillance of public places like parks is essential. Parks should not be fronted by garages, car parks, or the sides rather than fronts of buildings. Instead spaces around public places like parks should front the park directly and engage with it. This dignifies the park space, acknowledges its social value, and increases security.

Jan Gehl, author of *Life Between Buildings,* draws correlations between the quality of the urban environment, the types of activities that take place and the degree of social interaction. He found that 'necessary activities' that are more or less compulsory, such as going to school or work, took place no matter what the quality of the environment. He found that they do not necessarily lead to increased social capital. That is because there are limited opportunities for lingering. 'Optional activities', however, such as taking a walk to get fresh air or sitting and sunbathing, only took place when the weather was favourable and conducive to this type of activity. In this instance, there was a greater likelihood of social interactions. However, it was dependent on irregular optimal weather conditions. On the other hand, he argues that 'resultant activities' or social activities only take place in high quality public spaces that are designed to invite people to stop, sit, eat, play and so on. For example, a cul-de-sac or a homezone on a housing estate provides the opportunity for ball games and water fights among children and interaction between neighbours on a more regular basis.

A number of key qualities for successful public spaces, include key design features that affect the possibilities of meeting, seeing and hearing people.

- Spaces that are accessible and easy to move through to anyone who desires access without barriers to any groups either physically or symbolically
- Spaces that are legible in lay-out and design, with clear and recognisable routes, defined edges and clarity about the boundaries between public and private
- Spaces that are distinctive, locally relevant, designed with local character and the community in mind through participation
- Spaces that are open-ended, without exclusive domination of singular and incontestable cultural messages
- Spaces that are safe and welcoming, give the idea of comfort and a degree of control, with, for example good lighting and sight lines, and paying attention to different groups' needs with regard to safety
- Spaces that are not over regulated but which rely on natural surveillance and active use for safety
- Spaces that have features, such as a fountain, greenery or seating, that attract visitors to the place

The Psychology of Designing Public Space

People have psychological needs of public space. Public space can be a sensory, delightful, and comfortable experience. How a space is arranged in relation to surrounding uses, how it takes advantage of natural factors, and how street furniture is located creates a space that is inviting or repelling.

A number of the psychological factors identified are as follows:

- Space dimensions: The dimensions of squares should be correlated with the range of the 'senses' and the number of people that can be expected to use the spaces. Gehl uses the scale of the market stall to give a sense of scale that provides the most intense experience. He writes, 2 to 3 metres, is the size that permits pedestrian traffic, trade on both sides, and a clear view of the merchandise on both sides.
- The design of surrounding facades provide possibilities for influencing the concentration of activities and the intensity of experience for passersby. The concentration of activities depends on active and closely spaced 'exchange zones' between street and façade. Short distances between entrances and other functions contribute to activating the public environment with movement in and out.
- Sight lines are important. If people do not see a space, they will not to use it. In principle it is a bad idea to attempt to assemble activities by placing them above one another on different levels. Look out points can be placed high up but not activities that one wishes to assemble.
- Integration of various activities and functions in and around public spaces that allow people who work and live in the area to mingle and meet.
- Being able to see what is going on in public spaces also can be an element of invitation. For example, children who can see the street or playground from their homes are more motivated to go out and play. Merchants tend to locate themselves and display their goods where there is the highest footfall and visibility. Similarly, outdoor cafés works as a direct invitation to join in.
- Short, pleasant and manageable routes between the private and the public facilities makes public space inviting to use.
- A public space should have motive for people to seek it out

naturally. Destinations can be outings to particular places, lookout points, places to watch the sun set, or they can be shops, community centres, or sports facilities, etc. Having more than one motive attracts more people.

- Design for places for people to stand. Popular zones are along the edges and facades. Or in the transition zone between one space and the next making it possible for people to view both spaces at the same time. The reason for the popularity of the edge zones is that standing on the edge of a space provides the best opportunity for surveying it, manage distance between other people, and manage how much exposure they have. When a person's back is protected, others can approach only from the front, making it easy to keep watch and to react if need be. The doorstep between the façade and public space is always a good place to linger because people have choice whether to go further into the space or not. Christopher Alexander in *Pattern Language* summarises the experience of the 'edge effect' and 'edge zones' in public spaces when he writes: 'If the edge fails, then the space never becomes lively' because events grow inward, from the edge toward the middle of the public spaces.
- Public spaces that have colonnades, awnings, and sunshades along the facades are also attractive places for people to linger and to observe while remaining unobserved. For residences, niches in the façade, recessed entrances, porches, verandas, and plantings in the front yards serve the same purpose.
- Designs for places to sit provide the best opportunities for the numerous activities that are the prime attractions in public spaces: eating, reading, sleeping, knitting, playing chess, sunbathing, watching people, talking and so on.
- In designing seating, the edge effect influences choices of sitting places such as in niches, at the ends of benches, or at other well-defined spots. Sitting in places where one's back

is protected are preferred to less precisely defined places. Positioning benches in the middle of a space, floating freely, offers poor seating. Each seating area should ideally have its own local quality. For example, seating should be located in a small space within a space, a niche, or a corner. It should be a place that offers intimacy, security, and a good microclimate. Christopher Alexander encouraged the design of horseshoe shaped seating at the scale of a kitchen table to promote conversation.

- The location and scale of trees should be closely related to sitting spaces. The tree provides a satisfying enclosure; people feel cuddled, and protected, very much as they do under an awning of a street café.
- Seating should be positioned to take advantage of what the place offers. For example, activities in the space, views, weather, or all of these factors at once are important. Well-protected places to sit with an unobstructed view of the surrounding activities, are always more popular than the places offering fewer advantages and more disadvantages.
- In addition to well-positioned seating of benches and chairs, there should be opportunities for supplementary secondary seating in the form of stairs, pedestals, steps, low walls, boxes etc. that are needed for times when the demand for seating is particularly great.
- How to maximise the benefits of the weather can increase the time people linger in a space. Ways to hoard the sun, to double its light, or to obscure it, or to cut down breezes in winter and induce them in summer are important factors. Any design of a public space must take into account sun movement and wind studies. Trees planted along pavements and in open spaces can help reduce the negative effects of weather.
- Water in a public space can greatly enhance it. Water effects how we feel because of how it looks, feels and sounds. Water should be accessible, touchable and splashable.

- The presence of food in a public space creates activity. Outdoor cafés, street food vendors, mobile tables and chairs, when concentrated together provide a tight space for meetings and conversations while queuing or weaving through tables.
- Street corners are important meeting points and should be well-designed to accommodate social life. Whyte observed the activities that take place at the street corner; people will be waiting for the lights to change so they can cross; some will be fixed in conversation; others in prolonged goodbyes. If there is a street vendor, people will cluster, creating self-congestion. A well-designed street corner would not be walled off. It would have a front row position of prime sitting space to draw people and pull them into the public space.

Designing the Identity of Public Spaces

For public spaces to be inclusive, they should be open-ended, without exclusive domination of singular identity, and incontestable cultural messages. A number of ways in which public spaces can benefit from the richness of the area's cultural heritage is to create design interventions that can be enjoyed by all. The potential that fusing and hybridizing design traditions poses for areas is immense. It can produce something fresh and new, provide colour, forms and patterns that are vibrant and attractive. Hybrid designs offer a shared sense of collective identity. Every culture can see something of its heritage being incorporated in to their place.

A number of examples have successfully integrated diverse design heritages into their schemes. In Chumleigh Gardens in Burgess Park, London, a World Garden has been planted and landscaped to reflect the diversity of the surrounding population. The Oriental, Mediterranean, African and

Caribbean, Islamic and English gardens each contain a wealth of plants and design elements reminiscent of the regions and cultures they represent. The Oriental Garden has a calm, still pond and rock garden that contrasts with swaying bamboo-like foliage and tea bushes from the mountains of India. A more tropical feel is in the African and Caribbean garden with big leaved plants, cacti and succulents from drier regions. The Islamic garden is more geometric. Mosaic, lily pond and jelly palms form the centre piece of this enclosed fragment of paradise. Mediterranean gardens create shade and conserve water. Vines climb pergolas, and there are herb beds of grey leafed, drought resistant plants. The English garden provides a grassed space and tea room amidst the delights of the colour-rich English Garden borders.

Image of Chumleigh Islamic Gardens

Image of Chumleigh Mediterranean garden

Chumleigh Gardens is a focal point for many intercultural horticultural activities. Elders from the Asian, Irish, Afro-Caribbean and Vietnamese/Chinese communities are active. Groups of `Heart Gardeners', referred by their GPs, use raised beds and polytunnels for growing organic food, herbs and medicinal plants. Events such as the World Village Festival bring together Growing for Healthy Living groups. People with mental health problems benefit from the therapeutic benefits of the garden.

Image of Chumleigh tropical garden

Lister Park in Bradford, an important historical park, introduced a new key feature into its landscape design. The Mughal water garden was designed to reflect the rich Asian cultural heritage of Bradford. The garden is designed to tie in with Cartwright Hall. Although the building itself is in a rather different Victorian `Rococco' style, the two are not unsympathetic towards each other, using the same pale-coloured local stone. The garden has won awards for its enhancement of the use and visitors to the park. The design is based on key Mughal design principles. The use of the geometries of the square or rectangular are popular. Horizontal planes, terraces arranged in a symbolic hierarchy, symmetry, linear paths and avenues of trees are some of the key design features. The focal point is an arrangement of canals edged with stone, in which water cascades over carved chutes. Trees, such as plane and cypress, emphasise the lines and create a background to rose beds bordering the streams. The overall effect is one of complete calm and delight.

Image of Lister Park Mughal Garden

The gardens are inclusive by virtue of the many intercultural activities that take place at Cartwright Hall and the park itself. A Walking for Health group meet up, Arabic dance classes for women take place in the Bowling Pavillion and conferences, festivals, cultural celebrations, and exhibitions are held in Cartwright Hall. Activities include storytelling, turban tying, music, dance, theatre, body art, crafts, poetry, food stalls and a bouncy castle.

Image of Lister Park Cartwright Hall and Mughal garden

Markets: Shared Intercultural space

For a public space to be intercultural it should operate as a shared space. A shared space could be those spaces in which people from different cultures and walks of life co-habit. These are spaces where people spend time, such as gardens, parks, libraries, street markets and festivals. They don't necessarily create new acquaintances or conversations. Therefore the second quality becomes important, and that is diverse users are encouraged to interact with each other. Activity programmes, design, or events aids this. When shared space stimulates interaction between groups then this induces a sense of belonging.

Public markets in the open air or indoor, including farmers' markets and crafts markets, have sprung up in many cities today. Public markets are making a comeback. The reasons for this revival are diverse. Markets bring consistent activity to public spaces and can transform streets, squares, and parking lots. Public markets are valued because they create common ground in the community. People feel comfortable to mix, mingle and enjoy the serendipitous pleasures of strolling, people-watching, and shopping in a social environment.

With the recent economic crash, public markets have supported local economic development and small businesses. Markets become the sites for the exchange of fresh fruit, globally diverse foods, crafts and personal services that are often not available elsewhere at the same quality, variety and price. A public market creates a public space that is inviting, safe, and lively. A place that attracts a wide range of people. As an effective place where people mix, a public market can become the heart and soul of a community. The idea of the public market can be found across many cultures, making it a recognizable and familiar place. Public markets today are considered a solution to the ubiquitous indoor shopping malls that have attracted people away from the city's outdoor public spaces. Markets bring vitality and are an authentic glimpse of a city's unique culture.

In their interview-based study of the diverse neighbourhood of Newham in London, Dines and Cattell highlight the importance of markets as key spaces that are valued by different cultures. Queens Market is a bustling, jostling market, which facilitates casual exchange and encourages encounters between different cultures who would otherwise not come into contact with each other. It is generally recognised as a setting for developing tolerance. The design of the market provides spaces to linger without being moved on. People have the choice to browse or buy, giving the freedom to just stroll.

Image of Queens Market where diverse people meet

Mean and Tims in their study of co-produced public spaces describe the public experience of a car boot sale. People reported there was a high incidence of bumping into people they knew and chatting. There was no pressure for them to consume anything. This made people feel comfortable to spend the day with strangers. Regular stall-holders provided a familiar point of contact and common interest around certain goods such as antiques, toys, or books. They also reported people enjoyed the novelty of the experience, not knowing what or who they would come across. The relationship between vendors and buyers in markets provides a personalised experience where bartering is the norm. It is a good way to build social interactions.

Pop-Up Public Space

During the recession, many cosmopolitan cities were thinking of creative ways to maintain the vitality and vibrancy of public spaces. The Pop-Up movement was born. Empty shops, urban voids, and underused public spaces were programmed with temporary uses until the market picked up again. One particular pop-up campaign has been met with great success. In San Francisco, the Pavements to Parks programme was launched. The programme is a collaborative effort between the San Francisco Planning Department, the Department of Public Works, and the Municipal Transportation Agency. They recognised that 25% of the city's land area was made up of streets and public rights-of-way, more space than all the public parks combined. They identified excessively wide and underutilised areas, particularly at intersections. The programme tested inexpensive ways of converting these underused areas into new pedestrian spaces. Seating, landscaping, and paving treatments are common features of all projects. Design interventions are meant to be temporary and easily reversible, however, some spaces are reclaimed permanently as public open spaces.

Image of San Francisco's Pavement to Park Programme

Experimenting with Social Innovation: Co-design of Afrikaanderplein, Rotterdam

The Afrikaaderplein in Rotterdam is an inspiring story of how a run down, disused and vandalised park has become the heart of a culturally diverse community. The success of this park is the result of active involvement of different groups of local residents in the design of the space. Originally a working class neighbourhood, the multi-cultural Afrikaanderwijk was mainly inhabited by the city's dockworkers. One hundred and twenty seven nationalities can be found in the neighbourhood. Of the local residents 85% are from cultural minority communities including Turkish, Moroccan, Surinamese, Antillian, and Cape Verdian.

Afrikaanderpark is the only large open space in what is otherwise a very dense built up urban area. As a result it is an important resource for a number of different local community groups and stakeholders. The park incorporates a large open green space surrounded by trees. Three sides of this area are intensively used. A twice weekly market – Afrikaandermarkt – is the fourth largest in the Netherlands. The market takes place around the perimeter of two sides of the park and attracts 30-40,000 visitors each week.

The development of the Afrikaanderplein took place over a period of four years. Prior to its development the park was already being used by a number of different activities including the market, youth and sports groups, and the mosque. However these many and often conflicting uses resulted in a lot of tensions between different user groups. It led to the park being divided up into lots of different compartments without any proper planning. Rubbish, crime, security, poor drainage and maintenance were all major issues. The council of Feijenoord decided to tackle the problem, sending representatives to speak to local people and talk about how they would like to improve the area.

Image of Afrikaanderplein winning design
based on intercultural consultation

OKRA was commissioned to design the public space. OKRA launched an intensive interactive community engagement programme. The intensive programme included interviews, conversations and workshops with various neighbourhood organizations. This encouraged active involvement of local residents through the organizations. The workshops provided a shared space to increase knowledge, to improve attitudes and behaviour of residents, and to promote social cohesion between residents from diverse backgrounds. The working group included representatives of all the neighbourhood organizations, municipal services and the designers. The working groups were divided in to various thematic working groups such as design of playground, the bird sanctuary etc.

This engagement process resulted in different groups creating their own 'wish list' that helped OKRA in identifying solutions to the challenge. Intercultural group discussion and the sharing of knowledge during the participatory planning process was negotiated in relation to conflicts, budgets, operation and maintenance costs, etc. The result of the process was the creation of a robust design brief meeting the needs of the diverse community. The Housing and Urban Development Service and Department of Public Works became involved in developing the technical programme of requirements. OKRA undertook analysis of the spatial constraints and potentials of the square. A joint workshop with local residents, interest groups, designers, administrators and officials of the municipality resulted in a master plan for the redevelopment of the square.

Image of Afrikaanderplein with safety features

The key features of the design of Afrikaanderplein are:

- High accessibility and visibility. The perimeter is clearly demarcated with an open border (loosely-spaced trees, an attractive fence and gate, opening hours) to provide sight lines into the square and free flow of circulation around periphery and across the park by providing pedestrian paths

- An open layout design for flexibility to introduce a range of activities. The design combined uses for free and fixed functions which are complimentary and reinforce each other. The concept of the design of the park is a free central area surrounded by a framework of specific functions. Fixed functions (playground, botanic garden, aviary, and area for open market) are placed at the edges while free functions in the central area.
- The quality of the square and its street furniture is high with detailing of planting, new building and playground equipment, the botanic garden, and bird rescue centre.
- A strong image of the neighbourhood was created by employing new and existing functions. The lawned areas of the park were preserved and landscaped with different types and colours of plants with different arrangements. A water feature was placed between the mosque and park to provide clear definition of space. A lighting system was installed by the water feature and the open-air stage for performances.

Former tensions between different groups regarding the use of the park have been minimised by designing for flexible use, and also incorporating clear zones for different types of use. Noisy sports and play areas for children are situated along one side of the park. Whilst the water feature with a single bridge ensures that the mosque and botanical gardens have a more tranquil setting. This provides the mosque with a greater degree of privacy. The use of water as a boundary ensures that there is no visual barrier and thus the mosque can still be seen as an important part of the park. Barbecue sites have been created on one side of the park in response to a request from the Turkish community. Good lighting and fencing around the park has helped improve security and keep rubbish from the market apart from the green space of the park. The schools and local youth groups using the park include young people from a variety of different cultures. Their active use of the facilities in the park ensure that a significant degree of intercultural mixing takes place.

Proper management of the park ensures local concerns are addressed and activities are organised. This encourages intercultural understanding and social mixing. Local groups and users of the park meet regularly to discuss concerns and organise activities around key issues. Several cultural events are held in the public space and are held in conjunction with some of the major stakeholders, like the mosque holding Olympic Games to address issues of health and language.

The concept of the transformation of Afrikaanderplein is simple: Interactive and intensive community engagement prior to the design of a public space builds community cohesion. It results in public space being owned by all sectors of the community.

A critical attraction to Afrikaanderplein is the market. The market in particular is a prime example of intercultural mixing. Stall holders include Asian, Turkish, Moroccan, Dutch and other cultural groups selling everything from foreign vegetables and clothing to Dutch herring. Some vendors have a fixed stall, others are start ups, and others have stalls without a fixed place. Visitors are equally mixed. The level terrain and wide isles between the rows of stalls also enables parents with buggies and those in mobility vehicles to easily navigate around the market. The market has many advantages because of its marginal, off-centre location. It has free car parking in the neighbourhood, cheaper storage space for vendors, cheaper prices for items on sale compared to other open markets in the city. The market has been branded as a 'multicultural market: a place to meet and eat'.

Image of Afrikaanderplein market – a successful intercultural place

A particularly innovative engagement with the market led to Jeanne van Heeswijk setting up Free House – a project based on inclusive urban development through community participation and self-organisation. Free House has tested new plans for the market and successfully set up several communal workshops. Local people, and particularly women, develop their skills within this neighbourhood co-op to improve their access to the market with novel ideas. This locally-based co-operative aims to modernise the market by local branding within an existing multicultural exchange of ideas and experiences between entrepreneurs, young people, artists, and designers. This project has received worldwide publicity as a new form of micro-urbanism catalyzed by cross-cultural ideas.

What the example of Afrikaanderplein has shown is that co-production of the design of space can benefit the area socially, culturally, economically and environmentally.

Co-design of Afrikaaderplein Social Innovation Checklist

This section aims to determine where the social innovation in this project lies. The aim is to provide a benchmark for how to activate your public spaces in your neighbourhoods.

- *Does the co-design of Afrikaanderplein provide a product, service or model that addresses pressing unmet needs to improve people's lives and provide the solutions to social cohesion?* Yes. Co-design of the public space in Afrikaanderplein provides a model aimed at addressing the concern of an unsafe, vandalised and underused park. The tensions and conflicts over the use of the public space between different cultural groups was undermining social cohesion.

- *Does the co-design of Afrikaanderplein start from the presumption that people are competent interpreters of their own lives and competent solvers of their own problems?* Yes. The intensive and comprehensive public engagement process involved people from all cultural groups in the area to have an opportunity to create their visions for the public space.

- *Does the co-design of Afrikaanderplein lead to new or improved capabilities and relationships and better use of assets and resources?* Yes. The design brief of Afrikaanderplein was a culmination of the intensive public engagement programme and included functions and activities that addressed different cultural and social needs. The Afrikaanderplein market is now trading on its multicultural brand and providing economic opportunities for cultural minorities in the neighbourhood and for those engaged with Free House.

- *Was the co-design of Afrikaanderplein driven by a sharp external push that galvanised the will to change?* Yes. Tensions and conflicts in the different uses and users of the public space resulted in an underused, unsafe, and unloved public space.

- *Did there emerge a strong internal capacity to develop innovations and put them into practice through the right leadership, structures and organisational culture?* Yes. The working group represented the various cultural communities in the neighbourhood and they all had an equal say in the design of the public space to meet their needs. There was strong leadership by the local council in supporting the public engagement process.

- *Did the working group mobilise the right external resources by galvanising stakeholder support, partnerships and funding and mobilising a set of networks to embed change?* Yes. They sought funding from the EU and have put in place a public space management team funded by the local authority.

- *What was the nature of citizenship engagement in relation to understanding needs and problems, understanding larger patterns and trends, co-developing solutions and crowdsourcing solutions?* The nature of citizen engagement was based on local understanding of the problem and wider trends, and co-developing solutions through the planning and design process.

- *To what extent has the project completed the social innovation cycle: addressed critical issue; developed several approaches; mobilised teams to pilot approach; mainstreamed to scale up; disseminated to other fields and sectors?* Co-design of public space is a practice that can be transferred to other public spaces. Similarly the key principles of design can serve as a guide to creating robust public spaces that provide clear zones for different types of activity to minimise tensions which might otherwise occur. It may not have been disseminated to other fields and sectors due to appropriateness.

Chapter 7
Streets are Places

"As children get older, this incidental outdoor activity....becomes less bumptious....The requisite for any of these varieties of incidental play is not pretentious equipment of any sort, but rather space at an immediately convenient and interesting place. The play gets crowded out if sidewalks are too narrow relative to the total demands put on them. It is especially crowded out if the sidewalks also lack minor irregularities in building line. An immense amount of both loitering and play goes on in shallow sidewalk niches out of the line of moving pedestrian feet."

Jane Jacobs

Streets are public spaces that provide a pleasant and enriching experience. Streets have two key purposes; link and place. The link function is about movement. One part of a neighbourhood is connected to the other. Streets form an integral part of the whole urban street network. They are also spaces for the integration of urban transport networks like trams, bus or cycle networks. For people using the link function of streets, the primary requirement is to follow a continuous, linear path through the street network with minimum disruption. A seamless connection from one street to the next and from the beginning to the end of a journey. In general, linking seeks to minimise travel time by passing through streets as quickly as possible. Streets become movement corridors and the experience can still be pleasant and enriching.

The Place function, on the other hand, is when the street becomes a destination in its own right. The uses and facilities that align the street are what attract people on foot. They are destinations that provide the reason for pedestrians to spend time and carry out a wide variety of activities. Streets are places where people like to be, to walk, to shop, to meet, to play, and even to people-watch. The most successful streets are those that are easy to cross. Pavements become places for children to play and parents and grandparents to watch over them and socialise. People can walk with ease and safety to local facilities like the library, theatres, markets, and train stations. Yet many of these place functions of the street are being eroded.

Streets hold vast social, commercial, and political significance as powerful symbols of the public realm. They shape our physical and mental landscapes. We name streets after idols and fallen heroes. They are places for both celebration and rebellion. A street can become the stage for summer street parties and parades, and they can also be the place to gather to express public dissent as was seen in the London riots. When streets function well on the level of everyday experience, they provide opportunities for people to connect in a way that no other public space can.

Successful streets possess the following qualities:

- Activity and interest at the street level - people can walk, talk, look around, sit, stand and go about their business in a setting where they feel like they belong. Instead of blank walls, there are windows displaying merchandise, people inside, and places to sit.
- A comfortably scaled street is narrow with fewer lanes of traffic
- Slow moving traffic and on-street parking - the vehicle traffic is in balance with pedestrian activities. Parking spaces are available and not intimidating.

- Ample pavements – there is room for people to walk and for other pedestrian-friendly activities like outdoor cafés
- Image – the street has a character that identifies it as a special place. It is easy to cross and there is a feeling of safety

The effect of traffic on the social life of streets

When streets do not function well, the quality of life decreases considerably. The disappearance of streets as places has diminished in direct correlation to the increase in car usage. Streets have become hostile places. People are experiencing difficulties getting around their neighbourhood, crossing streets and make the social connections that were once possible when streets were quieter. Mothers find it difficult to take their kids around in a push chair; parents wonder whether it's safe for children to play on the streets or even walk or bike to school; and older people are feeling isolated because they don't drive.

In a famous study, Appleyard and Lintell demonstrated the dramatic effect of traffic levels on social relations. They studied three neighbouring streets in San Francisco with different levels of vehicular traffic. In the street where there was only little traffic (2000 vehicles per day), a great number of outdoor activities were registered. Children played on pavements and in the street. Entranceways and steps were used widely for outdoor seating. An extensive network of neighbour contacts were noted. Another neighbouring street where the traffic volume was greatly increased (16,000 vehicles per day) outdoor activities became practically non-existent. Comparably, neighbour contacts in this street were poorly developed. In the third street, with middle to high traffic intensity (8000 vehicles per day), a surprisingly great reduction in outdoor activities and neighbour contacts were noted, emphasizing that even a relatively limited deterioration of the quality of the outdoor environment can have a disproportionately severe negative effect on the extent of outdoor activities. It is claimed that since the 1990s the distance a child was allowed to venture alone from their home was nine times less than it had been 20 years ago. Traffic is detrimental to bridging social capital. Walking has became risky and the friendly quality of streets has disappeared. Impersonal streets dominate and take over the spaces where people used to meet each other. The focus on accommodating the car and the priority for moving traffic efficiently has led to wider streets, higher speed limits, traffic signals favouring the motorist, and narrower pavements.

Beyond traffic and safety issues, the loss of the place function of streets is having other negative impacts. For example, obesity and chronic disease is a result of less physical activity like walking. Social isolation and depression is down to a lack of access to good places, particularly for older people. Air quality has been degraded with increased vehicular emissions. Due to lack of transportation options, many communities have uneven access to jobs, social services, healthy food options, and community interaction.

Street safety

The absence of people walking and the lack of activity has made streets unsafe places. Newman in his book on *Defensible Space* argued that the heavier the pedestrian traffic the more enhanced is the sense of security. He claimed 'streets provide security in the form of prominent paths for concentrated pedestrian and vehicular movements; windows and doorways, when facing streets, extend the zone of residents' territorial commitments and allow for the continual casual surveillance by police in passing cars.'

Jane Jacobs held similar views. She supported city streets having more strangers, as they were a safety asset. In her view there were important factors that kept streets safe:

- A clear demarcation between what is public space and what is private space
- 'Eyes upon the street' of those natural proprietors of the street
- The buildings on a street are equipped to handle strangers and to ensure the safety of both residents and strangers, must be oriented to the street. They cannot turn their backs or blank sides on it and leave it blind.
- The pavement must have users on it fairly continuously, both to add to the number of effective eyes on the street and to induce the people in buildings along the street to watch the pavements in sufficient numbers. People entertain themselves watching street activity.

An inspiring example of how a street was activated is the case of a 'bench that built a community' in Mississauga, Ontario in Canada. Dave Marcucci recognised that his neighbourhood required a social renaissance. He began by tearing down the fence in the corner of his front garden. He landscaped the area and constructed a bench. His neighbours were intrigued by what he was doing and he received a number of comments. After he had finished, he threw a street party and invited everyone over. He invited everyone to use the bench whenever they wanted. Soon, everyone in the neighborhood was coming by to sit on his bench. Older people stopped to rest on it during their evening strolls. Children sat there as they waited for the school bus in the morning. Families out for a walk used it to take a breather. Soon his bench had created a friendly atmosphere in the neighborhood, introducing him to neighbours he didn't know and people he had never met. When he sat out on the bench, people would walk by, stop and talk to him. The bench was so popular, the next door neighbour added his own bench for the neighbourhood to use. What surprised Marucci most of all was the bench did not get vandalised or attract any negative uses. Such a simple intervention could transform the street and create the opportunities for lingering and chatting.

The High Street

The traditional high streets plays a central role in people's lives as the site of the everyday. High streets function as multiple-use centers, places to meet friends and family, and places to shop and be entertained. With the recent recession hitting high streets badly, the importance of the high street for the local community is under threat and with it, social cohesion. Several government-backed and community-led schemes have supported start up businesses and artists to occupy vacant shops. These schemes have demonstrated the social innovations focusing on how to draw people back in to the commercial centre. The focus has shifted from high streets as a place for convenience shopping to a place to visit; a destination in its own right.

The questions raised have been;

- What are the multiple uses and activities that attract people for different reasons?
- Do they meet the needs of diverse communities?
- Do these multiple uses support the routine and serendipitous encounters between different social, cultural and economic groups?

The questions are crucial to addressing the impact of economic failure of high streets and the loss of social cohesion. Increasingly, town centres and high streets are starting to consider a diversity of uses that can keep the high street vibrant throughout the day and evening. Places like theatres, museums, cinemas and restaurants can stay open late and counter the tendency for bars and clubs to dominate. During the day, other entertainment-based activities are being programmed to encourage longer staying times and to compliment shopping. It is crucial that the high street as a major commercial and community hub be a truly mixed use and diverse experience. That way it will regain its critical role in social cohesion. High streets should provide spaces where people can stay, sit and watch the world go by, at no or low cost.

New models for traffic calming

There are a number of new movements to slow traffic speed down with the aim to balance the needs of pedestrians, bicyclists and motorists. Traffic calming helps foster attractive places and welcomes all kinds of activities and serendipitous chance encounters. Appleyard and Lintell's study demonstrated the dramatic effect of high levels of traffic on the reduction in outdoor activities and neighbour contacts.

The Woonerf Movement is a Dutch innovation that is now global. It started by residents of one neighborhood being fed up with cars racing along their streets, endangering children, pets and peace of mind. One evening they decided to do something about it. They dragged old couches, planters and other objects out into the roadway and positioned them in such a way that cars could pass but would have to slow down. In a woonerf, the street is shared among pedestrians, bicyclists, and vehicles; however, pedestrians have priority over cars. The street is designed without a clear division between pedestrian and carriageway (i.e., no continuous curb), so motorists are forced to slow down and travel with caution. Limiting vehicular speed not only improves residents' feelings of safety, but also promotes greater use of the public space. This action allows more room for new features in the street. Street furniture like planters, street trees, and benches are areas for social interaction. It brings more people out on the streets to walk, bike, play, and interact with each other. In other words, a woonerf transforms the street into a livable and attractive environment for a variety of activities.

In a woonerf, use of traffic calming design elements such as seating, street lamps, bollards, and trees are positioned to create narrow roads. Elevating crossings to slow traffic and assert pedestrians' right to cross the street are installed. Woonerfs (Dutch for "living yards") became very popular, marking a shift from vehicle dominated roads to streets being a shared public space. Streets belong to people on foot and bicycles, in buggies and wheelchairs. Local Councils were at first skeptical of this grassroots initiative but residents took direct action without getting the council's permission. The concept is simple. It is to change the way streets are used and to improve the quality of life in residential streets by designing them for people, not just for traffic. Once the concept had been tested, the council then adopted it. Today it is a global movement in cities. Studies have shown the considerable increase in outdoor activities, particularly children playing and increased neighbourly interactions in woonerfs.

Another form of shared space is also being tested in cities worldwide. The concept of Shared Space was developed by a Dutch Traffic Engineer, Hans Monderman. He argued that engineering improvements to streets designed to make them safer were in fact doing the opposite. He observed the conflicts between the different users of streets was the result of heavily regulated signage, traffic lights, pavements, and crossings that did not give users the choice to behave responsibly. His concept was simple – remove the plethora of signage, traffic lights, and lanes, so people would stop looking at signs and instead start looking at each other. Monderman studied how more eye contact led to more measured decision-making by motorists which ultimately led to less accidents.

Shared Spaces differ from woonerfs in their prioritization. In Shared Space all modes are considered equal whereas in the woonerf pedestrians are given priority. In most cases of Shared Spaces, there is no differentiation or level-difference between pavement and carriageway. Design elements such as trees, bollards and street lamps, are positioned within the street to guide different users, and are far less prescriptive. Pedestrian zones are generous and allow for free movement across the space at any point. Traffic does not exceed 20mph limits.

What Shared Space offers is a basis for addressing safety issues. It overcomes community severance. Shared Space tackles congestion and enhances economic vitality in streets. By integrating pedestrians into the street as a place through which traffic is flowing slowly, crossing is made easier. Opportunities for human activity is enhanced. Shared Spaces provide the conditions for people to stay longer. The slow moving traffic does not dominate the street. Wider pedestrian zones provide greater opportunity for standing, sitting, and gathering, and greater freedom to use the street. The consequence of traffic calming is the increase in social interaction and cross-cultural encounters. However, Shared Space implies more than simple design techniques. It is a highly contested concept in many cities. Shared Space requires an innovative approach to the process of planning, designing and decision-making. As many cases have shown, implementing a Shared Space creates new structures for local government and public involvement that may not have existed before. Conflicts between users is the primary concern, particularly the visually impaired. However, there have been many successful examples.

Experimenting with Social Innovation: City Repair Intersection Project, Portland, Oregon

The City Repair Intersection project is a particularly inspiring story of Mark Lakeman's journey from corporate architect to founder of a community-led street reclamation movement. Mark lived in Sellwood, a leafy suburb of Portland and was struck by how empty the pavements were. He never met anyone. Most people drove when they had to go anywhere. The streets were empty of children. Only cars cutting through the neighbourhood on their way to downtown were using the streets. Mark realised that the highly uniform urban street grid so famous in American cities was at the source of the problem. Designed as a product of colonial parcelisation of land, the grid later becoming an efficient way of moving vehicles at medium to high speeds. The grid was killing off social encounters and interactions. For Lakeman, the imposition of the grid by 'the authorities' had a profound effect on the people who had to inhabit it; it estranged people from the process of shaping their own world. He identified the problem. The street layout did not support a sense of community. People were not taking control of the shape of their community.

His response to this concern was simple. Lakeman and a few of his friends built a ramshackle tea house of salvaged wood and old windows around the base of an old tree on his parents' property on the corner of the intersection of Southeast Sherrett and Southeast Ninth. They invited the neighbours to come for tea. Curious, people from up and down the blocks popped in. By summer, there were hundreds of people stopping by. This led to conversations between neighbours that had never existed before. One evening the crowd pushed right out into the middle of the intersection. The cars stopped and some of the people started to dance in the warm evening air.

Image of a City Repair intersection

Portland's Bureau of Buildings ordered the tea house, an unauthorised structure, torn down. Neighbours saw this as an opportunity to make a stand for their public space and their community. Thirty neighbours gathered one weekend in September and they brought paint. They began to coat the asphalt in concentric circles radiating from the manhole at its center so that all four corners were linked. From then on, the intersection would be a piazza. They called it Share-It-Square.

Image of communities getting together for City Repair intersection

Initially, Portland's Office of Transportation threatened to fine the neighbours and sandblast the circles off the street. But Lakeman built a strong case for his neighbourhood and the need for a truly civic space for the community. Within a few weeks the square had a conditional permit. The community went on to build a telephone booth–size library on one corner of the intersection so people could come and trade books. They built a message board and chalk stand on the northeast corner, and a produce-sharing stand on the southeast, and a kiosk on the southwest with a big thermos that they agreed to keep full of hot tea. Gradually neighbours began to open up their front gardens. They pulled down their fences and encouraged their neighbours to help themselves to vegetables from their produce stand. One neighbour built a community sauna. People began to help each other with their chores, exchanging tools, sharing childcare duties, and hosting neighbours for dinner. People have reported how many more friends they have made meeting at the intersection. Others have described how they were once scared of walking the streets because they didn't recognise or trust people they encountered. The tea house helped dispel those myths.

The idea caught on elsewhere in Portland and spawned the movement known today as City Repair. Dozens of neighborhoods in Portland and elsewhere have now staged their own intersection retrofits, with remarkable results. A Portland State University study found that the interventions create a blast radius of happiness for blocks around. After piazza-fication, people claim that their lives feel easier. They sleep better. Rates of depression fall. So do the number of local burglaries and assaults. The survey revealed that more than 85 percent of residents felt that communication between neighbours had improved.

A new city ordinance was passed with the help of City Repair. This kind of project can go forward if 80 percent of people within a two-block radius of an intersection consent. People may choose to do an intersection repair because they want a place for community interaction and seasonal celebrations, or simply because they want to slow traffic. Intersection repairs vary from neighborhood to neighborhood. One community may decide to paint a giant mural on the intersection and stop there. Another may go through many phases: painting the street, installing a community bulletin board, building a mini-café on a corner, reconstructing the intersection with brick and cobblestones, opening businesses to make it a village center. The results have been dramatic.

Today, City Repair holds an annual ten day Village Building Convergence event. It is a carnival that brings together skills, knowledge exchange, tea and food. Each day the convergence happens at sites all around the city (sometimes up to 40 sites). Neighbours come together with visitors to create community spaces that feature public art, gathering places, permaculture gardens, and natural buildings. In the evening, communities gather for an inspiring conference, community meeting, and music festival.

City Repair Intersection Project Social Innovation Checklist

This section aims to determine where the social innovation in this project lies. The aim is to provide a benchmark for how to activate your public spaces in your neighbourhoods.

- *Does the City Repair Intersection Project provide a product, service or model that addresses pressing unmet needs to improve people's lives and provide the solutions to social cohesion?* Yes.

City Repair transforms intersections from spaces dominated by vehicles with low levels of social encounter into places full of dynamic indoor and outdoor spaces that build communities. It is a model of reclaiming public space for community building.

- *Does the City Repair Intersection Project start from the presumption that people are competent interpreters of their own lives and competent solvers of their own problems?* Yes. City Repair is a community-led initiative where communities are claiming their public space to address the lack of community and social interactions in their neighbourhood.

- *Does the City Repair Intersection Project lead to new or improved capabilities and relationships and better use of assets and resources?* Yes. City Repair created new capabilities within communities wanting to address the social decline in their neighbourhoods. New relationships have been created between neighbours, and between residents and the council. City Repair makes better use of intersections as public space, a community asset.

- *Was the City Repair Intersection Project driven by a sharp external push that galvanised the will to change?* Yes. The City Repair Project was driven by a will to change the lack of social interactions in a neighbourhood in Portland.

- *Did there emerge a strong internal capacity to develop innovations and put them into practice through the right leadership, structures and organisational culture?* Yes. Mark Lakeman founded the City Repair movement that has become an annual practice. His social enterprise supports communities in taking action. City Repair organises the Village Building Divergence event annually as a structure for civic action.

- *Did the social enterprise mobilise the right external resources by galvanising stakeholder support, partnerships and funding and mobilising a set of networks to embed change?* Yes. A simple intervention of building a tea house at the intersection attracted neighbours and instigated conversations about action. Lakeman was able to demonstrate the value of his idea to transform intersections to the local authorities which led to a city wide ordinance supporting his initiative. Now that strong community bonds have been created, costs for painting are fundraised by the community. Several sponsors and stakeholders are providing funding.

- *What was the nature of citizenship engagement in relation to understanding needs and problems, understanding larger patterns and trends, co-developing solutions and crowdsourcing solutions?* The nature of citizen engagement was based on local understanding of the problem and wider trends, and co-developing solutions through the community-building, planning and painting process.

- *To what extent has the project completed the social innovation cycle: addressed critical issue; developed several approaches; mobilised teams to pilot approach; mainstreamed to scale up; disseminated to other fields and sectors?* Co-design of public space is a practice that can be transferred to other public spaces. The City Repair movement has been transferred to several cities in the US. As a model, City Repair still appear to have sole management of the delivery of the model. Therefore, mainstreaming, scaling up and dissemination has not yet happened.

Chapter 8
Friendly Neighbourhoods

"Under the seeming disorder of the old city, wherever the old city is working successfully, is a marvelous order for maintaining the safety of the streets and the freedom of the city. It is a complex order. Its essence is intricacy of sidewalk use, bringing with it a constant succession of eyes. This order is all composed of movement and change, and although it is life, not art, we may fancifully call it the art form of the city and liken it to the dance — not to a simple-minded precision dance with everyone kicking up at the same time, twirling in unison and bowing off en masse, but to an intricate ballet in which the individual dancers and ensembles all have distinctive parts which miraculously reinforce each other and compose an orderly whole. The ballet of the good city sidewalk never repeats itself from place to place, and in any once place is always replete with new improvisations."

Jane Jacobs

Neighbourhoods are the places of everyday life. They are the places we wake up in and the places we go to sleep in. Neighbourhoods are important. Where we grow up effects our life chances. Environmental psychologists and human geographers have documented that people are deeply affected by place. The environment has a profound impact on human behaviour and feelings. This book has focused on many of the key areas of everyday life in a neighbourhood; our interactions with neighbours and strangers, the public spaces where we encounter others, the everyday facilities and services we need to support our lives, and the activities that attract us to us other people. The book has also analysed the variety of circumstances and willingness of people to engage with each other. Understanding what is at the basis of social innovation, it is clear that people are motivated to engage with others when there is cause. Jan Gehl says 'social interaction or lack of it, is primarily conditioned by whether there exists an economic, political, or ideological sphere of interest in common among the residents'. I would argue there is a social dimension. Fundamentally, people attract people when there is a shared experience that is enjoyable, relaxing and engaging to bring them together. There is also the opposite. People living parallel lives is a reality for many people. That is why the social innovation projects discussed in this book were founded out of a common challenge or concern about the lack of socialising.

This chapter on Friendly Neighbourhoods discusses those physical, or designed factors, that could lead to greater social interaction. But as Gehl argues: 'spatial forms cannot be the propellant in social relationships. This does not negate the statement: The physical framework and the functional and social partitioning of the space can open up or cut off opportunities for development. It is possible to equip housing complex with a varied selection of communal facilities. It is possible to direct inhabitants into certain activity patterns through arrangements like access to dwellings through communal spaces, placement of building groups, and the like. It is possible to design the physical structure to contain areas and facilities that appeal to all residents or to groups of inhabitants. But this is also the limit to what the architects can do with regards to planning for how social life is to develop in the residential area.' In other words, design is only a setting for social life. What will attract people to a place is the setting. However, more importantly enjoyment, a common purpose, security and social belonging is the motivator.

The Physical Framework of the Neighbourhood

There have been many commentators who have described the demise of social life in cities as a result of modernist planning. Characterised by zoning and segregation of land uses, planning streets primarily for the efficient movement of traffic, and dismantling the traditional street and urban block layout; modernist planning has had a bad name. Greater distances between people, events, and functions has dramatically reduced the number of social possibilities. Several theories have since emerged to revive the urban patterns of historic towns and cities. They remain lively and vibrant places by the sheer intensity of people using public spaces. The New Urbanist Movement, in particular, have developed a neighbourhood concept that has been widely credited.

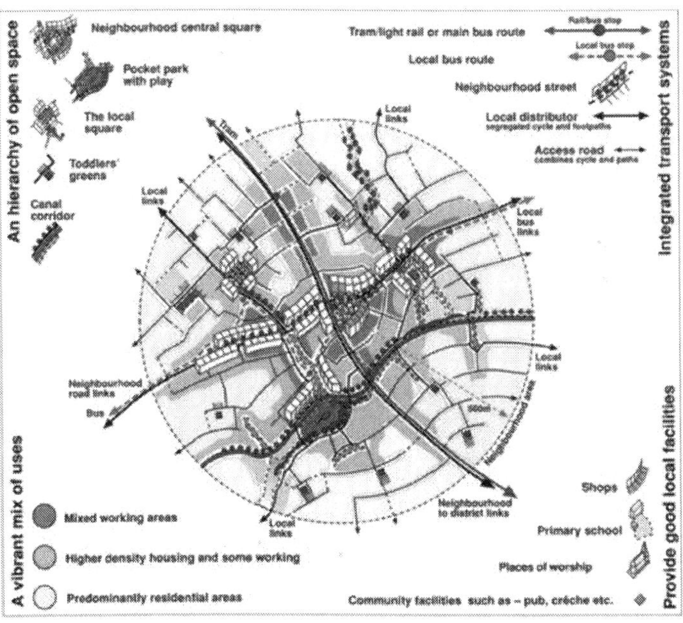

Image of a sustainable neighbourhood model

The model neighbourhood concept developed by its two largest proponents, Duany and Plater-Zyberk's, is characterised by:

- Compact, pedestrian-friendly, mixed use and identifiable areas that encourage citizens to take responsibility for their maintenance and evolution
- Daily living activities within walking distance, allowing independence to those who do not drive
- Appropriate building densities and land uses within walking distance of transit stops, permitting public transit to become a viable alternative to the automobile
- Interconnected networks of streets, encouraging walking, reducing the number and length of vehicular trips, and conserving energy
- A broad range of housing types, and price levels, bringing diverse ages, cultures, and incomes into daily interaction
- Concentrations of civic, institutional and commercial activity
- Schools sized and located to enable children to walk or bicycle to them
- A range of parks

Diversity is inherent in many of these principles. Spatial diversity as well as proximity of people from diverse backgrounds. Emily Talen in her book, *Design for Diversity*, is more specific. She identifies a number of reasons why planning and design of the built environment are critically important for social diversity. 'First, diverse neighbourhoods tend to have high number of physical transitions. Juxtaposition of difference are visible because in a diverse place there are different kinds of people doing different kinds of things. This can often be the cause of stress, particularly since the meaning and implication of various physical elements can get accentuated in diverse neighbourhoods: boundaries can take on special significance, connectivity can clash with heightened need for privacy, or visual coherence can conflict with diverse tastes and styles.' In her view, design can act as a catalyst for focusing people's attention on the public realm. If neighbourhood issues are framed in civic terms, residents may be motivated to think about their similarities and connections rather than their differences and conflict.

Talen puts forward three strategies most relevant to social diversity; mix, connection and security.

- Mix includes housing mix and mix of services and facilities. Mix of housing relates to mix of housing types, housing ages and affordability levels. She considers the importance of codes and policies to govern and manage the location of housing mix. The transition between areas with different housing types should be through the design of open spaces and streets. In relation to a mix of service, high levels of diversity can be accommodated in the presence of smaller land plots for smaller businesses. Smaller plots are often called 'fine urban grain'. Larger plots, or coarse grain, can be accommodated by wrapping the larger buildings with more fine-grained development. Finer grained development generates greater levels of activity.
- Connection promotes connectivity in the street network, establishing the '100 percent corner' where multiple activities can coalesce. Providing services and facilities as shared spaces to foster cross-cultural connectedness. Connecting all types of spaces; public and private, residential and non-residential, shops and pavement. Enhancing connectivity can be achieved by prioritising the pedestrian over the needs of vehicles.
- Security can be addressed by housing integration, surveillance, activity and edges. New housing developments should not be walled off or insular. There should be an opening or connection to the neighbourhood. Surveillance

can be enhanced by buildings fronting on to the public realm. People should be able to look out of their windows directly on to the public realm. Similarly, around parks and other public spaces, buildings should be fronting on to them. Activity should be introduced in the dead zones of the neighbourhood such as the parking lot or vacant land. Streets should be lined with active uses. Edges can help define the boundaries and identity of a neighbourhood, however, they can also be negative such as a highway or barren industrial landscape. Buffers can protect harsh edge conditions by greenways, or adding resilient building types such as offices or light industrial buildings.

Other design strategies can also be considered in neighbourhood design:

- Size is often expressed in relation to population or comfortable walking distances of 400metres or 10 minutes, or a combination of both. Identifiable neighbourhoods don't necessarily correspond with people's social relations, nor do residents necessarily perceive a neighbourhood unit as such. Several studies of people's perceptions of a neighbourhood have found three types: the 'social acquaintance' neighbourhood; the 'homogeneous neighbourhood'; and the 'social provision' neighbourhood. Most congruent with people's social relations is the social acquaintance neighbourhood that included a small physical area associated with the third places, or 'hang outs' where they go.

For Jan Gehl, a simpler repertoire of interventions would support or discourage social contact. Gehl focuses on five different strategies that enhance human senses and promote or prevent isolation or contact. Isolation is promoted by: Walls, Long distances, High speeds, Multiple levels, and Orientation away from others. Conversely, contact is promoted by: No walls, Short distances, Low speeds, One level, and Orientation toward others.

The different neighbourhood models discussed rely on a top-down planning and design process. In contrast, there are some commentators who believe the best neighbourhood concept is one that is supported from the bottom-up, citizen-led. A number of key actions foster a sense of shared community:

- Create places where people can stop to sit and chat with each other, such as putting a bench out in front of your house
- Tame traffic in neighborhoods by making streets so interesting that people naturally slow down to see what is going on.
- Develop new activities for teens that make them want to get involved in the future of their neighborhood instead of feeling excluded and alienated from the community.
- Introduce new kinds of park activities, such as gardens catering to certain groups - for example, children, seniors, or various ethnic groups, or a bread oven that is used to cook community dinners.
- Improve safety and security in a neighborhood by encouraging people to do things like saying hello to everyone they see. This can change the spirit of a community faster and more effectively than a police presence will ever do.
- Bring new kinds of people to the local neighbourhood centre with creative campaigns that deliver social and economic benefits for the place.
- Promote new opportunities for social interaction and community pride by introducing activities from different cultures, such as bocce ball courts, casitas, or an evening promenade.

- Make kids healthier by developing innovative programs so they can safely walk or bike to school.
- Establish more effective community-based planning processes that result in less arguing, more public input, and a general level of agreement on what to do to make the community better.
- Foster new types of businesses that not only make money but also have more far reaching impacts — for example, rent fun and unique bikes to people who don't ordinarily ride bikes, like seniors, disabled people, and young children.
- Champion the local hangout by making it a 'Third Place' such as a coffee shop, café or other spot where everyone feels welcome and can strike up a conversation with their neighbours.
- Provide clean public restrooms through enterprising programs that grow out of partnerships between businesses and the neighbourhood association.

The recent shift in citizen-led micro-urbanism is now considered the most socially-innovative way to regenerate neighbourhoods. This is not to negate the importance of understanding the key principles of the physical framework of a neighbourhood. However, the proposition is that local people are experts in their neighbourhoods. Their involvement in co-producing public space is access to the vibrancy and liveliness of a successful neighbourhood.

Citizen-led micro-urbanism

The power of markets to attract people across all cultures has already been identified. Allotments and food growing are another strong attraction for people of different ages and cultures. Today, a number of worldwide movements have started to consider the health benefits of green spaces and food growing. The Transition movement and guerilla gardening are just some examples. Food growing provides the basis for sharing cultural identity, customs, recipes, and healthy eating activities.

The Norris Square Neighbourhood Project is an inspiring example of how a number of people from a local Latino neighbourhood set up the project. They wanted to promote their culture to the wider community and to encourage collaboration and intercultural exchanges. Founded by Natalie Kempner, a local fifth grade teacher, and Helen Loeb, a professor at Eastern University, they collaborated with a dedicated group of volunteer teachers, artists and community residents named Grupo Motivos to found the Norris Square Neighborhood Project. Together they created an educational center. It was culturally relevant to and protective of the children living in West Kensington, Philadelphia, notorious at the time for its deadly drug culture. They negotiated with the council the use of a number of urban voids in the neighbourhood and turned them into gardens.

The environmental and cultural education programmes have helped transform the surrounding community and the lives of Latino Norris Square residents. The project provides youth programming, community engagement opportunities, and a culturally-themed gardening programme. There has been a strengthening of intergenerational relationships between children, parents and grandparents as they have learned and grown food together. One of its keys to success is its accessibility. Norris Square has made its space welcoming to people and groups from both within and outside of the local area.

The theory of community change that the Norris project is driven by focuses on supporting the children. They will affect change in their house, and then expand to their school, block, street and subsequently, their community. Their youth engagement project has led to greater youth leadership and governance over the project. The impact of this work is the neighbourhood is a much safer place. People get along. The gardens that are run by the Norris Project have become third places where the community meets to share food, learn about food, and gain greater understanding about Latino culture in the neighbourhood.

Reaching the Hard to Reach Neighbours

In diverse neighbourhoods one of the most difficult hurdles to overcome is bringing people together across all cultures. It is not uncommon that cultural groups feel disengaged from mainstream society if there is a weak sense of belonging, despair, or discrimination. At the start of any neighbourhood project, it is this mindset that first needs to be addressed if any form of community building is to take place. Local institutions such as community centres, faith centres, collectives, businesses, and housing providers may be the first port of call to invite diverse people to the table.

More creative engagement could be delivered through public art. One example is the Splash of Colour programme of temporary public artworks developed by the architects practice, Shillam + Smith Urbanism. Their commission was in response to the early challenges of an urban regeneration scheme in Saltley, in Birmingham. What they found was the 'area had little cohesion, few landmarks and a confusion between its Victorian and quintessentially British past and the modern, overwhelmingly Asian present'. They felt that in order to address the process of regeneration successfully and in order to find new meaning for these areas they had to tackle the issues of multiculturalism.

They undertook a series of surveys in the area and from this they were able to obtain major concerns from the local population. These included the mismatch between new housing development and housing need, problems of traffic congestion and environmental decay, a fear of crime and a need for more community and cultural activities in the area. They also noted that the cultural diversity of the area was not manifest in the architecture or environment. What they had first distinguished as a characterless neighbourhood was in fact a function of the relative newness to the area of many of the people who lived there; those who had come from South Asia have been trying to assimilate their traditional lifestyles with a Victorian infrastructure and with modern British culture. Nowhere had anyone attempted to understand this synthesis or to respond to it in the mechanics or in the aesthetics of the regeneration. People had not yet had the opportunity to assert their identity and as such they felt no ownership or responsibility for the public domain.

Shillam + Smith commissioned six artists to create six temporary consultation projects. David Cotterrell's installation examined public space. Cotterrell was interested in creating a piece of public work capable of transcending language barriers. Like the party atmosphere of a Brooklyn summer, when fire hydrants are tampered with to allow water play, Cotterrell's 30 metre inexplicable water 'geyser' served as a meeting point for the local community of Couchman Road Park. Local residents gathered in the park to witness the event. Within days of its installation, news of the 'phenomenon' had spread, and people were making an effort to meet at the geyser in order to chat, catch up on gossip and watch their children play in the water. This public green space was in a state of decline: many residents avoided the park as there seemed to be constant supply of burnt out cars decorating its landscape. But the same people responsible for various acts of vandalism took ownership of

Cotterrell's geyser; keeping the site secure became de rigueur for local teenagers in the months their geyser was operational. The 'geyser' was a starting point to bring people out of their homes to enjoy the spectacle, to start conversations, and to make people think about how their open spaces could be used.

Image of David Cotterell's 'geyser'
public art installation attracting people

Image of David Cotterrell's 'Geyser' started conversations amongst neighbours

The Internet of Things and the Sharing Economy have become new ways of community building. The use of social media tools and the power of the internet is a way to bring people, goods and services together. Numerous sharing platforms have been created to build neighbourhood one-stop-shops. One of the fastest growing innovations is Bright Neighbor in the US and its sister platform, Compare and Share in the UK. Bright Neighbor started off in a neighbourhood in Portland, Oregon. Bright Neighbor combined community involvement with social tools that helped local governments, communities, and businesses increase livability, sustainability, and relocalisation while simultaneously improving local economies. Users can map important resources in the community, schedule private and public events there, start an inventory of skills and items available for hire or exchange, and more. The aim is to promote community cohesiveness, maximise resource use, and lower the carbon footprint of residents through an online hub that facilitates offline connections.

Image of Bright Neighbor website to give residents information about their neighbourhood

The concept is simple. It is based on aggregation. That is when companies offering competing sharing services are allowing their services to be marketed together in comparison marketplaces on one platform. For Bright Neighbor, they realised people looking to participate in the sharing economy were missing what's available in their neighbourhood if they didn't visit the right websites. Their response was to create a one-stop shop for all goods and services in any neighborhood. With Bright Neighbor people can search and see all their options in one place. The neighbourhood focus is a virtual space that leads to face-to-face encounters around shared interests. This is one way to tap into the increasing use of social media and the internet to reach more people in the neighbourhood. It has its disadvantages too, particularly for those people who are not currently participating in the digital movement.

Experimenting with Social Innovation: Woensel-West Neighbourhood Regeneration, Eindhoven

The Woensel-West regeneration project is a particularly inspiring story of how Trudo housing association has implemented a number of socially innovative projects to transform the negative reputation of the neighbourhood. Woensel-West is a neighbourhood in Eindhoven, Holland of 4000 inhabitants. The neighbourhood was built in the 1920s to provide housing for skilled blue-collar workers for the nearby Philips complex. Dramatic demographic shifts to the area began with the settlement of unskilled workers from Southern Europe, Turkey and Morrocco to work on the assembly lines of Philips and DAF. They were soon accompanied by their wives and children. The neighbourhood became less cohesive and social conflicts arose. Further conflicts in the neighbourhood were stemming from the long-established presence of prostitution and associated organised crime. Drug dealers occupied several bars in the neighbourhood, and people trafficking from the Caribbean, Africa and Eastern-Europe was taking place. Woensel-West built up a reputation as a 'no-go' area of criminal activity. Security became a major problem in the neighbourhood, not only for the women, but for children.

The neighbourhood was given special 'urban renewal status'. Central government provided additional funding for the renovation of accommodation, improvement of public spaces and the organisation of a wide variety of social activities. It failed partly because of the economic recession and especially the decline of Philips. Many people leaving psychiatric institutions were housed in the district.

The challenge for Trudo was being responsible for managing the transformation of the neighbourhood's reputation in a socially-sensitive way. They called their new approach a 'game changer'. Trudo consulted with the residents around the security concerns. There first action was to focus the prostitution around a square to the edge of the neighbourhood. The bars associated with drug trading and prostitution were closed down. People began to feel safer and to use the public spaces. Children began to play outdoors.

Dealing with the security issues has paved the way for a number of socially innovative projects to establish a new reputation for the area. The first one was connected to transforming the life changes of children. Trudo set up a mentoring programme. They invited students to settle in Woensel-West on the basis that they provide 10 hours of volunteering time to support local children in their homework and language skills in exchange for reduced rent. The pilot succeeded and the social mix of the neighbourhood changed. Students brought in a hip and creative vibe to the neighbourhood. Start-ups and social enterprises began to open up. At the same time, the schools in the neighbourhood have started to be one of the top performers in the Eindhoven.

Another strand of work was to transform the urban feel of the area. Many of the houses were looking dated and poorly maintained. Trudo set up a number of programmes. One programme was a graffiti programme to decorate houses to add some colour to the street. Another programme was a public art project run by the local collective of artists and designers, Aunt Netty, that engaged local residents in developing social connections. Some projects included a street poetry project where artists used boarded up houses as their canvas. The Woensoll Supertoll project collected people's hopes and dreams in a temporary art installation. One project, Pak n' Chair pays homage to the familiar white plastic garden chair which adorns many front gardens in Woensel. The chair is used to sit with neighbours and chat over a beer. The chair is literally used to come in contact with neighbours and thus stands for encounter. Stories and anecdotes were collected about their old garden chairs.

Image of Aunt Netty public art project to improve look of boarded up houses in Woensel-West

Trudo are not demolishing large numbers of housing but rather focusing on creating landmark architecture at the corner plots of blocks as public buildings and waymarkers. A number of these corner plots have been out to architectural competition. A focus on public spaces has also been key to changing the feel of the neighbourhood. One example is the demolition of one hundred houses as part of the master plan. Initially, the site would remain closed until construction began, but Trudo commissioned the artist Vincent Wittenberg to create a temporary project to the gap site. His response was inspired by the white picket fence so familiar in Woensel-West. He constructed an enlarged copy of one of the white picket fences with two gateways. This way, Wettenberg was returning the space back to the neighbourhood. Volunteers built the 180 metre fence. It resonated with its surroundings and in the recent past, it also became an object with its own qualities. An important result was the former gap became a temporary neighbourhood park. Several activities have been organised there including sports, arts, and crafts days for children, dinners and a festival. A group of volunteers constructed an allotment and an adventure playground. One summer, two Turkish women started a traditional tea garden with Rummikub music and shisha. People walk their dogs, others take short cuts and the place provides a safe place for children to play away from traffic.

Image of one of the entries of an architecture competition to create corner landmarks in Woensel-West

Image of public art installation around a gap site turned temporary park in Woensel-West

Interventions have also taken place in the new housing developments that are being built. One example is the Volta Galvani, designed by Geurst and Schulze. They have produced a design in close consultation with the residents. Referred to as a new style *qasabah,* the housing facades use references of colour, materials, proportions and design elements such as arches and patterns from Morrocco and Turkey, to create a 'multicultural' architecture. The quality of the architecture is contemporary, novel, and imaginative. The complex benefits from a shared hard-landscaped public space and a new row of shops where many of the new creative businesses have moved into. The Volta Galvani project is part of a larger masterplan that is being delivered by Trudo to change the image of the area. Festivals are bringing new visitors to Woensel-West.

Image of Volta Galvani housing scheme in Woensel-west inspired by Middle Eastern architecture

Although the unemployment, health problems and social cohesion issues in the area are still not fully addressed, Trudo is putting in place a long term vision. It is based on three pillars: empowerment so no one is left behind, particularly children; changing the image to create safety, social cohesion, enjoyable public spaces, and liveliness; and changing the reputation of the area to support employment opportunities for residents.

Woensel-West Neighbourhood Regeneration Social Innovation Checklist

This section aims to determine where the social innovation in this project lies. The aim is to provide a benchmark for how to activate your public spaces in your neighbourhoods.

- *Does Woensel-West Neighbourhood Regeneration provide a product, service or model that addresses pressing unmet needs to improve people's lives and provide the solutions to social cohesion?* Yes. Trudo provides a combination of services such as housing, education and employment support. Trudo also provides a holistic model of regeneration that combines social, environmental, physical and economic programmes in parallel. The aim is transform the reputation of the neighbourhood and improve the quality of life and life chances of Woensel-West residents.

- *Does Woensel-West Neighbourhood Regeneration start from the presumption that people are competent interpreters of their own lives and competent solvers of their own problems?* Yes. Trudo started its work with a comprehensive public consultation that identified security as the primary priority. Their work, through the use of social entrepreneurs, creatives, and other partners, is based on community engagement and co-production.

- *Does Woensel-West Neighbourhood Regeneration lead to new or improved capabilities and relationships and better use of assets and resources?* Yes. Trudo's strategy to invite new residents to the neighbourhood instantly created an opportunity for better community cohesion. Students supporting children to get ahead in their education in return for reduced rent was a great opportunity for mutual support. Trudo's partnership and collaborative approach uses local networks and businesses to co-produce the regeneration.

- *Was Woensel-West Neighbourhood Regeneration driven by a sharp external push that galvanised the will to change?* Yes. Woensel-West suffered from a bad reputation with high levels of organised crime and prostitution. The poor levels of security in the neighbourhood were a priority for residents and Trudo to work together.

- *Did there emerge a strong internal capacity to develop innovations and put them into practice through the right leadership, structures and organisational culture?* Yes. Trudo is an open organisation committed to the public good and to discouraging gentrification. The organisation has set out a clear vision to develop innovations in co-producing regeneration of the neighbourhood.

- *Did Trudo Housing Association mobilise the right external resources by galvanising stakeholder support, partnerships and funding and mobilising a set of networks to embed change?* Yes. Central government is a major funder.

- *What was the nature of citizenship engagement in relation to understanding needs and problems, understanding larger patterns and trends, co-developing solutions and crowdsourcing solutions?* The nature of citizen engagement was based on local understanding of the problem and wider trends, and co-developing solutions through the community-building, planning and design process.

- *To what extent has the project completed the social innovation cycle: addressed critical issue; developed several approaches; mobilised teams to pilot approach; mainstreamed to scale up; disseminated to other fields and sectors?* Trudo is operating at the neighbourhood scale in a custom-made approach to deal with the many problems the area has faced. It is unclear to what extent Trudo's experience is being disseminated nationally and internationally. It is also not clear if it is having an impact in other sectors such as the education sector.

Concluding Remark

Bridging Cultures has shown the creative innovations people have used to deal with the challenges of cosmopolitan cities. At the heart of this book is the message that public spaces provide critical settings for intercultural social encounters. The right social conditions, however, are required to activate public spaces. These conditions are based on activities and programmes that dispel prejudices and build tolerance. Without this first crucial step, public spaces will remain arenas of 'cultural indifference and civility' and not social cohesion. The lack of social cohesion has been proven to reduce the competitiveness of cities. It is the innovations that diversity brings that, if harnessed, can make the difference in the competitive edge of one place to the next. Bridging Cultures isn't just a nice idea. It is fundamental to the liveability, creativity and success of places. The case studies in this book show that social innovation is at the heart of social cohesion. Social innovations are about providing the framework for the flourishing of strong civic action and leadership. Cities need to provide an open, welcoming, and experimental framework for innovations to take root and transform the essence of society. A society based on values of trust, co-operation, and creative hybridisation.

Bibliography

Anna Minton (2012) *Ground Control. Fear and Happiness in the twenty-first-century city*. Published by Penguin

Andres Duany and Elizabeth Plater-Zyberk (2010) *Suburban Nation: The Rise of Sprawl and the Decline of the American Dream.* Published by North Point Press.

Ash Amin (2002) *Ethnicity and the Multicultural City: Living with Diversity. Environment and Planning.* 2(4), pp. 959-980

Caroline Holland, Andrew Clark, Jeanne Katz and Sheila Peace (Open University) (April 2007) *Social Interactions in Urban Public Places.* Published by The Policy Press for the Joseph Rowntree Foundation.

Charlie Tims and Shelagh Wright (2007) *So What Do You Do? A New Question for Policy in the Creative Age.* Published by Demos.

Christopher Alexander, Sarah Ishikawa, and Murray Silverstein (1977) *A Pattern Language.* Oxford University Press

Commission on Integration and Cohesion (2007). *Our Shared Future.* Published by The Crown.

Donald Appleyard and Mark Lintell (1972) *The Environmental Quality of Streets. The Residents view point.* Journal of the American Association 3892), pp. 84-101.

Edward Relph (1976) *Place and Placeness.* Published by Pion.

Emily Talen (2008) *Design for Diversity.* Published by Architectural Press.

Gordon Allport (1954) *The Nature of Prejudice.* Published by Addison-Wesley.

Hannah Lownsbrough and Joost Beunderman (July 2007) *Equally Spaced? Public space and interaction between diverse communities.* A Report for the Commission for Racial Equality

Iris Marion Young (1990) *Justice and Politics of Difference.* Published by Princeton University Press.

Jane Jacobs (1961) *The Death and Life of Great American Cities.* Published by Vintage Books.

Jan Gehl (2001) *Life Between Buildings.* Published by The Danish Architectural Press.

Jay Walljasper (2007) *The Great Neighbourhood Book. A do-It-Yourself Guide to Placemaking.* Published by Project for Public Spaces.

John M. Quigley (1998) *Urban Diversity and Economic Growth.* Journal of Economic Perspectives 12(2), pp. 127-138

Ken Worpole and Katharine Knox. (April 2007)*The social value of public spaces.* Published by the Joseph Rowntree Foundation.

Kevin Lynch (1960) *The Image of the City.* Published by MIT Press.

Lyn Lofland (1989) *Social Life in the public realm. A review.* Journal of Contemporary Ethnography 17, pp. 453-482.

Mandeep Hothi and Corinne Cordes (August 2010). *Understanding neighbourliness and belonging.* Published by The Young Foundation.

Matthew Carmona, Tim Heath, Taner Oc and Steve Tiesdell (2003) Public Places. *Urban Spaces. The dimensions of urban design.* Published by the Architectural Press.

Melissa Mean and Charlie Tims (September 2005) *People make places: Growing the public life of cities.* Published by Demos. Report available from www.demos.co.uk.

Nicholas Dines and Vicky Cattell with Wil Gesler and Sarah Curtis (Queen Mary, University of London) (September 2006) *Public spaces, social relations and well-being in East London.* Published by The Policy Press for the Joseph Rowntree Foundation. Report and summary available from www.jrf.org.uk.

Nicola Bacon, Nusrat Faizullah, Geoff Mulgan and Saffron Woodcraft (January 2008). *Transformers. How local areas innovate to address changing social needs.* Report Published by NESTA.

Oscar Newman (1973) *Defensible Space. Crime Prevention Through Urban Design.* Published by Macmillan.

Phil Wood and Charles Landry (2010) *The Intercultural City. Planning for diversity Advantage.* Published by Earthscan.

Project for Public Spaces (2008) *Streets as Places.* Published by PPS.

Ray Forrest and Ade Kearns (2001) Social Cohesion, *Social Capital and the Neighbourhood.* Urban Studies 38(12) pp. 2125-2143.

Ray Oldenburg (1999) *The Great Good Place: cafes, coffee shops, bookstores, bars, hair salons and other hangouts at the heart of the community.* Published by Marlowe and Co.

Richard Florida (2002) *The Rise of the Creative Class.* Published by Basic books.

Richard Sennett, (2004) *The City as an Open System,* Presentation at London School of Economics, Leverhulme International Symposium 2004 'The Resurgent City'. https://www.richardsennett.com/site/senn/UploadedResources/The%20Open%20City.pdf (Accessed 30 August 2015)

Richard Sennett (2005) *Civility. Urban Age.* Bulletin1, pp. 1-3.

Robert Putnam (2000) *Bowling Alone. The Collapse and Revival of American Community.* Published by Simon and Schuster Paperbacks.

Sara Ferlander (2007). *The Importance of Different Forms of Social Capital for Health.* Acta Sociologica Vol 50(2),pp. 115-128

Setha M. Low (2001) *The Edge and the Center: Gated Communities and the Discourse of Urban Fear.* American Anthropologist, 103 (1) pp. 45-58

Sophie Watson with David Studdert (Open University) (September 2006) *Markets as spaces for social interaction: Spaces of diversity.* Published by The Policy Press for the Joseph Rowntree Foundation. Report and summary available from www.jrf.org.uk.

Stephen Vertovec (2007) *Superdiversity and its implications.* Ethnic and Racial Studies 30, pp. 1024-1054

Susan Fainstein (2005) Cities and Diversity. *Should We Want It? Can We Plan For It?* Urban affairs Review 14(1), pp.3-19.

Susanne Wessendorf (2013) Be*ing open, but sometimes closed. Conviviality in a super-diverse London neighbourhood.* European Journal of Cultural Studies 0 (0), pp. 1-14

Suzanne Hall (2012) City, Street, Citizen. *The measure of the ordinary.* Published by Routledge.

Ted Cantle (2008) *Community Cohesion: A New Framework for Race and Diversity* Published by Palgrave Macmillan.

Tessy Britton (ed) (2010) *Handmade. Portraits of emergent community culture.* Self-published through Blurb.

Theodore Morrow Spitzer and Hilar Baum (1995) *Public Markets and Community Revitalisation.* Published by Urban Land Institute and Project for Public Spaces.

William H. Whyte (1980) *The Social Life of Small Urban Spaces. Published for Project for Public Spaces.*

Yi-Fu Tuan (1974) *Topophilia. A study of environmental perception, attitudes and values.* Published by Columbia University Press

Source of Images

Afrikaanderplein:

http://www.landezine.com/wp-content/uploads/2010/05/okra-afrikaanderplein-rotterdam-10.jpg

http://www.landezine.com/wp-content/uploads/2010/05/okra-afrikaanderplein-rotterdam-04.jpg

https://marketsinthetropics.files.wordpress.com/2015/06/afrikaanderplein-markten-in-rotterdam-2p-location1140c-0.jpg

Bright Neighbour:

http://i.ytimg.com/vi/SX4OozOJBI8/maxresdefault.jpg

Burnside Park:

http://www.pps.org/wp-content/uploads/2014/05/family-reading-time.jpg

http://www.pps.org/wp-content/uploads/2014/12/2014Storytime.jpg

https://exposure.imgix.net/production/photos/x2t49gr8zschm2t9vpwzx8c881vy4x6rnsat/original.jpg?w=800&fm=pjpg&auto=format

Chumleigh Gardens:

http://belowtheriver.co.uk/wp-content/uploads/2013/04/p045-Chumleigh-Gardens-1.jpg

http://belowtheriver.co.uk/wp-content/uploads/2013/04/p046-Bonnington-Square-7.jpg

https://trainwalkslondon.files.wordpress.com/2014/03/t37a_600x600_100kb.jpg?w=640

City Repair:

http://www.spontaneousinterventions.org/wp-content/uploads/2012/08/58crop.jpg

http://www.slate.com/content/dam/slate/blogs/the_eye/2013/11/12/131112_EYE_SHARE-IT-SQUARE.jpg.CROP.original-original.jpg

Lister Park:

https://c2.staticflickr.com/4/3742/18683607859_292572cb44_b.jpg

https://farm8.staticflickr.com/7093/7279943530_771650c4f6_o.jpg

Pavement to Park:

https://thosespacesinbetween.files.wordpress.com/2010/06/rebar_walklet-2010.jpg

PieLab:

http://farm5.static.flickr.com/4143/5412313826_6d0d4a5863.jpg

http://payload.cargocollective.com/1/0/14291/2051296/pielab_facade.png

Queens Market:

https://www.theimagefile.com/v/tp/119/349/1022627_4_queens-market-english-british.jpg

Saltley Geyser:

http://www.daniellearnaud.com/images/cotterrell/SaltleyGeyser01.jpg

http://www.daniellearnaud.com/images/cotterrell/SaltleyGeyser03.jpg

The Neighbourhood Model:

http://www.redtreellp.com/images/background/policies/The-Key-Components-of-a-Mixed-Use-and-Integrated-Urban-Neighbourhood.jpg

Woensel-West:

http://www.slimmerkopen.nl/uploads/clusters/6602.jpg

http://i.obstorage.nl/271206a3dccf489cb07033efc2dbb3b0/opener/Groot_werk_op_huis_Woensel-West_(Foto_Rogier_van_Son).jpg

http://www.urbansignature.nl/foto/tuin/sloopwijk.jpg

http://denkkamer.com/images/projects/woensel/denkkamer_architect_gemert_woensel_eindhoven_dJ4.jpg

Made in the USA
Charleston, SC
14 October 2016